The Miracle of Harley: What Every Rescue Dog Owner Needs to Know

The Miracle of Harley: What Every Rescue Dog Owner Needs to Know

Rose M. Murphy

The Miracle of Harley:
What Every Rescue Dog Owner Needs to Know

by Rose M. Murphy

First Edition
Paperback

Cover and internal layout design by zDogz Publishing, LLC

Publisher:
zDogz Publishing, LLC
39506 North Daisy Mountain Drive
Suite 122- No. 261
Anthem, Arizona 85086
Email: zdogzpublishingllc@gmail.com
Website: www.zdogzpublishingllc.com

The Miracle of Harley: What Every Rescue Dog Owner Needs to Know, by Rose M. Murphy
www.themiracleofharley.com

Book Design: zDogz Publishing, LLC

Editors: Elizabeth Macdonald and Yon Makino

Cover Photo: Melissa Young Photography
www.melissayoungphotography.com

Library of Congress Control Number:

ISBN 10: 0615519806
ISBN 13: 9780615519807

Printed and bound in the United States of America

Dedication

Dedicated to my parents Harold and Catherine, who have
been the greatest support in my life.

Sometimes in life events happen beyond reason and logic. They are unpredictable, unexpected, and call forth from within us decisions that shape our lives. This is a true story of such events.

Harley, December 2010

Author's Notes

Numerous animal rescue groups, shelters, and other types of organizations throughout the world, in addition to the ones mentioned in this book, should be recognized and commended for their value and contribution to ethical animal welfare and well-being. The statistics included in this book are based on research collected at the time of writing.

Table of Contents

Preface

Many families in America experience the joy of owning a pet. According to the Humane Society of the United States, 39 percent of American households own one or more dogs. Unfortunately, not all of these pet relationships are successful. The American Society for the Prevention of Cruelty to Animals (ASPCA) states that approximately five to seven million companion animals enter shelters every year, with about half ending up being euthanized. For dogs in particular, more than 20 percent of people who abandon them to shelters actually adopted them from a shelter. Why does this happen? What goes wrong in these pet relationships? According to the National Council on Pet Population Study and Policy, the top reason why dogs are relinquished to shelters is that the owner is moving. One surmises that the deeper issue revolves around owners having fewer resources in their new situation. Not surprisingly then, the next top reasons cited in the list do indeed concern inadequate resources for taking care of the dog – not enough time, not enough space, and the high expense of pet maintenance. Successful dog/owner relationships are founded both on having a clear understanding of dog behavior, and having realistic expectations of what is needed to properly care for the dog. For those who are getting a dog for the first time, this book can help you develop more realistic expectations of what is needed for loving dog care – touching on topics of space, training, and exercise - so that your dog can be healthy, well adjusted, and ultimately happy.

For people who are considering getting a rescue dog, or fostering one, this book can alert you to the unique challenges that you may face. For those who are experiencing the tragic loss of their beloved dog, may this book offer you solace and hope. Finally, for those of you who have never owned a dog, may this book reveal the joy and love that dog companionship brings.

Introduction

"Wisdom begins with wonder."
                                                Socrates

This is a story of wonder, transformation, and ultimately, a miracle. When I was twenty-six years old, I participated in formal training at the Capitol Area Humane Society in Columbus, Ohio to become a dog rescue worker. This local area humane society was committed to reducing the overpopulation of homeless animals. It offered a wide range of training both to people interested in volunteering at the animal shelter, and to those who wanted to do dog rescue work, assisting in finding homes for rescue dogs. Here, not only did I learn the basics of proper dog care, including canine nutrition, health, and safety, but I also became immersed in the art of dog rescue. This included how to greet individuals and families who came to the shelter looking for a rescue dog, as well as how to assess their requirements and expectations in order to create the best match possible.

Factors that influence this matching process include not only breed characteristics for both purebred and mixed breed dogs, but also age, size, exercise needs, and personality as well. In some cases, the individual or family asks for a recommendation on which dog would be best suited to their lifestyle. In other cases, the individual or family just wants to walk through the dog-holding area to see if one in particular catches their attention. Once a dog of interest has been identified, the shelter arranges a "meet and greet" where the rescue dog and prospective owners meet in a secluded, safe, and secure area at the shelter's location.

Humane societies and animal shelters across the United States work tirelessly at sheltering and finding homes for stray and lost dogs and cats. What is so important in this adoption process is establishing the right match from the very beginning, ensuring a lifetime commitment from the potential dog owner, and a forever home for the rescue dog. I was usually able recognize within the first few minutes of the "meet and greet" process if a bond or connection between the potential owner and the intended rescue dog was taking place. Individuals and families sense this bonding and connection as well, experiencing an instant knowing that this is their dog. Such moments are magical. In other cases, several visits to the society are necessary before the correct rescue dog match can be made. This training I received as a young adult helped to prepare me for the dog rescue work I would be involved with over the course of the next twenty five years.

Now, having successfully placed over a dozen dogs in my life, I recognize how important this dog adoption process is in our society today. That these dogs and strays, who have been abandoned or left without care or shelter for any countless number of reasons, are taken in and cared for, that they find their forever homes, makes our communities more compassionate and loving places. That so many abandoned dogs, even dogs with health or behavioral problems, are adopted into the homes of kind owners through the tireless efforts of animal shelters, humane societies, and rescue groups speaks volumes to the depth and promise of our human nature.

If you find yourself going through the process of adopting a rescue dog, be prepared for all the myriad of ways that adopting this dog will transform your life. Be prepared for that inexplicable instant of "knowing" that this is your dog, and trust it. The dog may not look like what you expected - he may be very large, or very small, or very hairy, or perhaps not hairy at all, but your heart will recognize him. Go with your gut feeling when meeting your dog, and let that experience enrich your life.

For me, the miracle of Harley is the miracle of transformation. As a child growing up with dogs that lived long lives, and were such an integral part of the family, I thought that their lives would always march in tandem with mine. I have since come to a different realization. Our dogs grow old, succumb to illness, and finally depart. But as they do, they help us to better understand and experience our ability to love and nurture, and help us to take enormous leaps of faith amidst confusion, fear and terrible loss. As our companion exits our world, it often presents unchartered waters, and yet we have no choice but to continue the journey and to trust in where it will lead. For me, the loss was so painful that I was convinced that having no dog was far better than getting another who could never replace the one I lost. And yet, here I am with my third dog. I have learned that each time, in accepting and honoring that instant of knowing, our capacity for loving is much greater than we ever imagined possible. Inexplicably, the exiting opens a pathway for others to enter in a way that, only in hindsight, reveals such a high level of perfection so as to seem predestined. This book is about a miracle in all its facets of transformation – that of commitment, love, trust, and faith - the miracle of Harley.

Chapter 1: Getting My First Dog, A Purebred Puppy

According to the National Council on Pet Population Study and Policy (NCPPSP), 25 percent of purebred puppies purchased as family pets end up being relinquished to animal shelters. The percentage of purebred puppies purchased that remain in their original home during their lifetime is only about 50 percent. One of the major contributing factors to pet relinquishment by their owners is poor general knowledge about animal behavior, leading to unrealistic expectations of their pet. My purebred chocolate Labrador retriever Teela and I were among the lucky ones. Looking back, I realize that our success was based on far more than luck, and that key factors related to understanding a dog's behavior and providing an environment that meets his needs play a role in successfully bringing a dog into your home.

When I was twenty four years old, my boyfriend gave me a puppy, whom I named Teela. She was only five weeks old when I brought her home. Before doing this, however, I had made it a point to meet both of Teela's dog parents. The people who bred Teela and her littermates lived with the dogs in their house as a family. I was fortunate to get to know both the dog parents and Teela's puppy siblings. Both of her chocolate Labrador parents were good looking, sturdy, healthy, and happy. They had their purebred papers from the American Kennel Club. "How special!" I thought at the time. I had the opportunity to see the house where the dog breeder family lived, the yard that Teela's parents played in, and the designated maternity area where Teela's mother nursed and slept with her puppies. From birth, Teela's puppy home was ideal. I didn't realize at the time how lucky I was to get a glimpse of where Teela lived for the first few weeks of her life, and the temperament that Teela was likely to inherit.

Teela, seven weeks old

Teela was the first dog that I had on my own as a young adult. Although my boyfriend had chosen her for me, we were a perfect match. When full grown, she weighed about seventy pounds, the right size for me - not too small but not so large that I couldn't control her physically. Growing up, my family always had a dog or multiple dogs. I felt well equipped with my knowledge and experience of having lived with dogs all my life. But very quickly, I learned that having a puppy could be challenging!

Some of the challenges I encountered included: how to potty train a puppy to go outside, how to develop a routine and daily schedule that both worked for me and addressed Teela's exuberant energy levels, and how to discipline and train a puppy in a healthy, positive, yet effective manner. Developing consistency in my role as the pack leader was a daily goal for me. Adding to the challenge was trying to balance the demands of raising a puppy with the demands of building a new career as an interior designer.

As Teela matured, I became familiar with the medical and health issues that needed to be addressed when raising a dog. My vet promptly initiated a puppy treatment plan for her to ensure she received the correct sequence of required and recommended vaccines. I kept track of her medical records and general puppy care. The vet also coached me on which foods to use for different stages of her development, when and how to worm, and how to prevent chiggers, ticks, mosquitoes, and heart worm from affecting her overall health. I even learned about the different types of poisonous plants common to the area. I soon purchased dog treats, dog collars, dog leashes, dog bowls, dog food storage containers, dog beds, dog seat belts for travel and even toys that could survive the extreme chewing tendencies of a Labrador puppy.

Teela was a chewer! Not only did I find out that the Lab breed typically does not reach maturity until the age of three or so, but also that this breed is noted to be among the most persistent chewers of home furnishings, clothing and accessories. When left alone, Teela chewed on beds, sofas, chairs, plants, sheet-rock, baseboards, and anything else of interest within reach in my home. Almost any object in the vicinity was free game. I had to be vigilant in keeping poisonous and toxic household cleaners and solvents out of her reach. I quickly learned that a puppy or dog without proper training won't make the distinction between an old pair of shoes given to them to chew, and an expensive pair of pumps that are off-limits. I needed to continually and consistently set boundaries with Teela. This chewing behavior had to stop. My entire townhouse, both inside and out, was showing scars and battle wounds from Teela's excessive chewing habits. In addition to the chewing, she propped herself up on the counter and would help herself to bread, butter, fruit and any other miscellaneous snack items within her reach.

The solution, my vet told me, was to purchase a crate for Teela. She said that a puppy could easily be overwhelmed having free run of the house. But, shutting her in the basement or bathroom is psychologically bad for the dog, giving them a panicky sense of being trapped. Instead, by providing Teela with her own secure, dedicated safe space, such as a dog crate that controlled her access yet allowed her complete visibility of her surroundings, I could provide her with a sense of safety and security, even when I was away.

At the vet's recommendation, I purchased a large heavy duty wire dog crate to use at times when I was away from home. The dog crate was secure on the top, bottom and all surrounding sides, ensuring that while she could not exit, she could still see out. I placed it in the family room by the sliding glass doors so that she could watch the outdoors and enjoy the daylight. Inside the crate, I placed blankets, a water bowl, and a piece of my own clothing so she would be comforted by my scent. I began by rewarding her with dog treats whenever she would enter the crate. In the beginning, I only left her in for short periods of time - fifteen minutes at the most – and eventually worked her up to hours at a time. Much to my surprise, she appeared to love her crate!

The crate training was such a positive solution and one of the most valuable things I learned in those first years of raising Teela. She would frequently enter her crate, checking for treats or curling up to take a short nap while I worked around the house. It taught me the importance of looking at the world from a dog's perspective instead of just mine. I saved myself thousands of dollars of house destruction from a bored, teething, Lab puppy.

The second most important lesson I learned about having a dog was the importance of enrolling in obedience classes. The dog training Teela and I received taught us about dog manners with people, and people manners with dogs. I learned how to set healthy boundaries and how to reward Teela appropriately. Together, we socialized with other dogs and their owners who were working to achieve the same goals. These lessons became invaluable to me over the years in the numerous social situations we encountered. I felt proud to have a dog that understood obedience and displayed well-mannered behavior when meeting new people and their dogs.

Teela and I shared many happy years together. She lived a full life, and experienced a natural decline in her energy levels and activities. At the age of 16, she passed away. I was very sad to see her go, and didn't consider getting another dog. I couldn't imagine replacing her, and was content to readjust to living without her.

In memory of Teela June, 20, 2001

Chapter 2: Getting My First Rescued Foster Dog

Almost two years had passed since Teela's departure. Even though I missed Teela's companionship, I honestly could not consider getting another dog. In my mind, no one could replace Teela, so I resigned to live without a canine companion. My life was full. Being young and single, I devoted most of my time to my flourishing career and to renovating the 1920's Victorian revival home that I had purchased six years earlier. While I missed the companionship of having a dog, and knew that my life was out of balance, I wasn't ready to get another dog.

One day, my friend and neighbor Ann dropped by my house. She held an advertisement clipped from The Atlanta Journal Constitution. The ad read:

"To Our Readers and Advertisers: Some persons who respond to these ads will not give a pet a good home. To ensure the pet's safety, check references and visit the new home shortly after the adoption. And please, remember to have your pet spayed or neutered. Your vigilance may save a pet from abuse.

LAB Chocolate, 1yr, fem, spayed/shots, needs fenced yd & tlc. Rescued. Call (phone number provided)."

Clearly the people who placed this ad wanted to be sure that those who responded to the inquiry were sincere about taking the dog in as a pet, and were not going to turn around and sell it to an animal research laboratory. The phone number turned out to be the number of a dog rescue group, even though they didn't identify themselves as such.

Despite my protests, Ann clearly saw the happiness a dog would bring into my life again. I began to reconsider. Sometimes when you can't rely on yourself to make a needed adjustment in your life - in this case getting a new dog - a friend or relative who knows you well enough can offer a helpful perspective.

Yet, the challenge was that I really wanted Teela back. After a few days of processing Ann's suggestion, I called the number in the ad to find out more about this dog. I was told that the dog, whose name was Olivia, needed either a foster or permanent home. When I heard "foster," I felt that this was the right match for me because while I wasn't ready to own another dog, I could certainly foster one and still get the companionship that I missed.

While adopting confers full ownership, fostering a dog means making a commitment with an individual, persons, or group, such as a rescue dog group, to provide temporary care and accept responsibility for the dog in your own home until a permanent one can be found. The duration of the temporary care can vary depending on the dog's physical and emotional states. In many cases, the animal will need time to rehabilitate. If the dog has been abused or neglected, extra time may be needed for its recovery. The vet will advise the foster home of the specific care needed during this time. This is what I agreed to undertake.

With mounting excitement, I went to the address in the advertisement to meet the dog in person. As I waited anxiously, volunteers from the rescue group released a dog from her holding kennel. My heart sank. I could see that she was underweight and her ribs bones prominently protruded through her chest. She gazed at me timidly and I noted she stood smaller than a standard Labrador Retriever. I suspected that she was mixed with some other breed - perhaps a German Short-Haired Pointer or even a pit bull. Her entire petite body was chocolate brown, except for a small quarter-sized white marking on her chest, a few white hairs on her front paws, and one white toenail on her back right paw. Though in need of attention, she was adorable, young, and energetic as Labs usually are. Purebred Labs are typically a solid color, but I took Olivia's white marking on her chest as a sign that she was the one for me to foster, and I felt I could give her the love and care she needed to prepare for adoption into a new permanent home.

I finalized the arrangements with the rescue volunteer and signed the legal documents for the State of Georgia, agreeing to accept responsibility for her foster care. The rescue worker also gave me medical documents detailing the treatments she had received at the vet clinic, and enough food to carry her through the next few days. I committed to taking her to monthly pet adoption events to meet potential owners. By placing her in my home environment, temporary though it would be, the rescue worker and I felt it would help her emotionally adjust to being with people again, and in so doing, make her more adoptable. I liked the short term nature of the foster care arrangement and was confident that this would work out well for both of us.

When pressed for more details of Olivia's history, the rescue worker confided that Olivia's past included more than a few foster homes, including one in which she suffered mistreatment by being locked away in a basement for long stretches of time. Consistent to all her foster home stays, she had not gotten along with any other dogs. When the rescue group had taken her to dog adoptions in the Atlanta metropolitan area, they had no success in finding her a suitable home.

Bringing Olivia home

In my new role as Olivia's foster parent, I knew that exercise was going to play a crucial role in her recovery. Physical activity would give her the opportunity to shed anxiety, fear, and pent-up energy. And certainly in Olivia's case, she carried all three in abundance. The first day, when I brought her home to her new temporary residence, she meekly walked through the front door, tail between her legs, sniffing cautiously from room to room around the house. I was careful not to overstimulate her, but instead to let her adjust at her own pace. After she acclimated to the new environment, I fed her, and upon finishing, she lay down and slept. Because she was quite underweight, she needed frequent small meals until she regained her normal weight.

I provided Olivia with her own designated "dog spot" or "dog nest" on the family room floor. This was how I oriented Olivia to my home. As the weeks went by, we established a routine of regular exercise, eating, playing, and sleeping, with lots of affection spread throughout. This was the pattern I had so often enjoyed with Teela and now grew to enjoy with Olivia. It felt comfortingly familiar to have this routine again.

But Olivia wasn't Teela, and I was surprised to find that some things were quite unfamiliar to her. For example, she didn't know how to use stairs, and in fact, seemed quite fearful of them. Living in a three-story town-home, and wanting Olivia to have full access throughout the house, this posed a problem. Training consisted of me taking her by the collar with one hand, and offering her treats with the other, gently coaxing her up and down the stairs. After, I would leave treats for her strategically placed several steps away to encourage her to explore on her own. Within a few days, she was confidently bounding the steps on her own, more occupied with finding treats than concerned over foot placement.

Olivia as a foster dog December, 2003

I noticed also that Olivia didn't play with toys and I realized she probably never had a dog toy before. Appealing to her retriever instincts, I crouched on the floor and shook a toy temptingly in her face, looking – I hoped – much like a canine companion in play mode – smiling, laughing, and play growling in excitement. Then throwing the toy, I would encourage her to chase it. As I hoped, her instincts surfaced and we were soon engaging in an enthusiastic game of fetch.

Olivia with her favorite toy

I found that while Olivia was very timid with people, she was extremely aggressive towards other dogs. One time, she even broke through the screen door and took off after a dog she spotted outside. Fortunately, I was able to catch her, but her behavior perplexed me as the other dog had done nothing to provoke or antagonize her. When I took Olivia to adoption events, she displayed these hyper-aggressive instincts towards other dogs – nullifying her chances of being adopted.

Over time, Olivia overcame her timidity with people, but her aggressiveness with other dogs was tenacious. She was like a canine version of Jekyll and Hyde. With me or with other people, she was loving and affectionate, by all appearances secure and stable. But when she saw or heard another dog, she would go ballistic! Because my house was located on the edge of a neighborhood that was being gentrified, there was constant noise of people and cars passing by. The house faced directly to a busy street, so Olivia could tell whenever a dog was passing by. When she did spot another dog, she would run frantically from one end of the room to the other, jumping on furniture and window sills, challenging the other dog through the window pane. Outside, when exposed to another dog, she would lunge on her leash, moving to attack. Even the friendliest, most passive dogs would set her into a frenzy!

This aggressiveness greatly concerned me and I resolved to address it. According to the ASPCA, aggression is the most common and most serious behavior problem in dogs, and is also the number-one reason why pet parents seek professional help from behaviorists, trainers and veterinarians. First I tried to resolve it on my own. Very assertive measures, such as using a choke collar with prongs and harsh voice commands had no effect on Olivia. When I asked my vet for advice, he didn't have any easy answers or solutions. He did, however, recommend a reputable local trainer, who had had success with other dogs and their disciplinary issues. Although it was quite expensive, I enrolled Olivia in his obedience program, feeling a surge of hope. In the first class, Olivia exhibited her typical hyper-aggressive behavior – growling, snarling, and lunging for the necks of any dogs nearby. The trainer took Olivia out of the room to calm her down, and confided that this was the most severe case he had ever seen. He sent me home with a workbook of dog exercises to practice with Olivia, providing us with an evening of mutually enjoyable interaction, given that there were no other dogs present. The next morning, the trainer called and apologetically explained that the other members of the class had complained about the danger that Olivia posed and he felt he had no choice but to refund my class fee and ask us to leave. He felt that Olivia's fear-based aggression would require special training, more than he was willing or able to provide.

At this point, I decided to research aggressive behavior in dogs. I found that canine aggressive behavior problems can be classified in different ways, depending upon the cause. For example, a dog may have territorial aggression where aggression is used to protect their territory, or they may have social aggression when aggression is used to assert their dominance. These and other types can be found on the

ASPCA website. In Olivia's case, her aggression appeared to be motivated by fear of other dogs. With this type of aggression, instead of trying to retreat from what they are afraid of, they instead initiate an attack, thinking that it's better to be the attacker than the one attacked. In her case, all dogs seemed to frighten her, and she would charge at them, barking and growling. She never showed aggression with people, only dogs.

Having exhausted all my options, I returned to the rescue group and pleaded for more information about her past, anything to help me better understand her temperament and behavior. The rescue group was initially reluctant to give me information, but I insisted and convinced them to dig up Olivia's original records to see if anything might shed light on her behavior.

Apparently, Olivia had been taken out of the mountains in Northern Georgia, and they suspected that she was between one and two years old when she came to live with me. When they found her, she presented the rescue group with a whole host of health issues. She had contracted heart worm, had a litter of puppies and was then sent to Atlanta by another rescue group. She had been diagnosed with an immune deficiency problem. She had pellets in her side, suggesting that she had probably been running loose in the woods and got shot. One of the rescue workers told me that Olivia had been used as a bait dog, as evidenced by scars on her head. "A bait dog?" I thought. Over my years of living in the South, I had heard that the barbaric sport of dog fighting still existed, but knew very little about it.

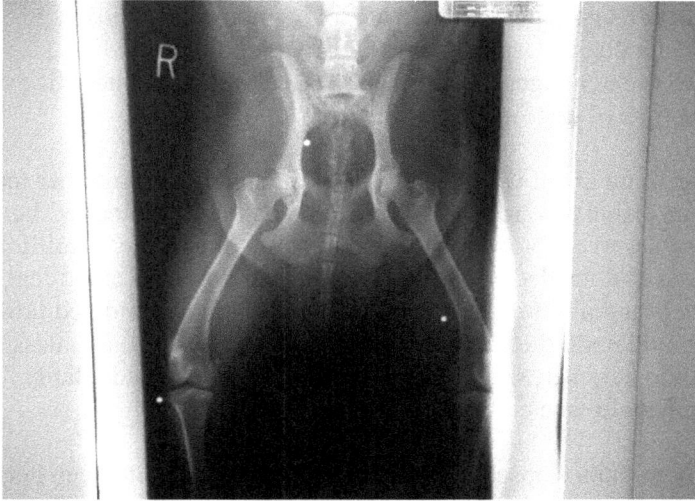

Pellet shot in Olivia's body

Simply put, bait dogs are used to test another dog's fighting instinct. Bait dogs are often inexperienced fighters who are used as practice fodder for more experienced and aggressive fighting dogs. Dog fighting is considered a blood sport since the dogs bite, tear, and use any manner of force to subdue the opposing dog, often incapacitating or killing it. Although illegal, the cruel sport of dog fighting has been reported throughout the country, from rural to suburban to urban areas alike. Oftentimes, admission fees are charged to watch a fight. Stud fees are charged to breed the fight victor with another. Gambling is common as people try to predict who will be the top dog.

Both fighting and bait dogs are usually kept in isolation until the actual fight. They are caged, crated or confined in some way, sometimes for days at a time before the event. Rarely are they given proper food and water. Unsurprisingly, these dogs are usually poorly socialized, both with other dogs and with people. In some cases, legal or illegal drugs have been forced upon the animals before the fight to intensify their aggressive instincts. Steroids are commonly used for this purpose and will increase muscle size as well. Narcotics are also used both to increase aggression and to mask the pain of injury from wounds, prolonging the fray, often until the death of one of the combatants.

Lost or stolen pets, some from loving homes, can be enslaved as bait dogs. Despite efforts by various groups and law enforcement agencies throughout the country, the horrific pastime of dog fighting still occurs.

Learning about Olivia's past helped me to understand her fear aggression towards other dogs. As a bait dog, somehow she had survived. Now, in addition to being one of the 70 million dogs that needed a home, she was a bait dog with emotional scars and nightmares of fighting for her life. I wondered how I could undo the horrors of her past. I knew now that unless I could help her, she would likely be viewed as unadoptable, and could face euthanasia.

Six months elapsed. I loved this dog and wanted to keep her forever, no matter what, bait dog history and all. I was committed to providing the medical care and training necessary to help Olivia become a well-balanced, healthy and happy dog. Knowing the truth of her past, I felt immeasurably protective of her. No one would ever hurt her again. Two years later, we left Atlanta and moved to the Southwest.

Chapter 3: Our New Beginning

The Southwest was ideal for me. While living in Atlanta, I had developed arthritis in my lower back and though manageable, the pain and discomfort was exacerbated by Atlanta's rainy weather and oppressive humidity. The Atlanta neighborhood I lived in was a bustling, urban tract bordering on a rundown section of town. I had witnessed two murders, I'd been stalked, and I had fended off several attempted break-ins. Finally, I decided I'd had enough. Since I had always dreamed of someday living in the Southwest, with its natural beauty, open desert, and dryer climate, now seemed like an opportune time. Eagerly, I sold my three-story, 1920's urban Victorian house in Atlanta and moved to a newer single-story stucco home in a quiet suburban community in the Southwest desert. This house was smaller, more manageable, and had a good-sized private yard, with plenty of space for Olivia.

Unfortunately, the next year proved challenging for Olivia. It became clear to me that the downside of adopting a rescue dog was that you could potentially inherit a host of medical issues with no knowledge of the dog's medical history to help troubleshoot what might be going wrong. Olivia's medical problems seemed to be unending, and we were regulars at the vet's office. She developed a mast cell tumor in her thoracic cavity, which fortunately did not metastasize. However, the surgery she underwent to remove this tumor was very invasive and involved a difficult recovery. After a full year, she developed another lump on her abdomen, palpable to the touch. The vet aspirated it, said it was likely cancerous, and recommended that it be removed. After the surgery to remove it, however, the vet determined that it was, in fact, benign.

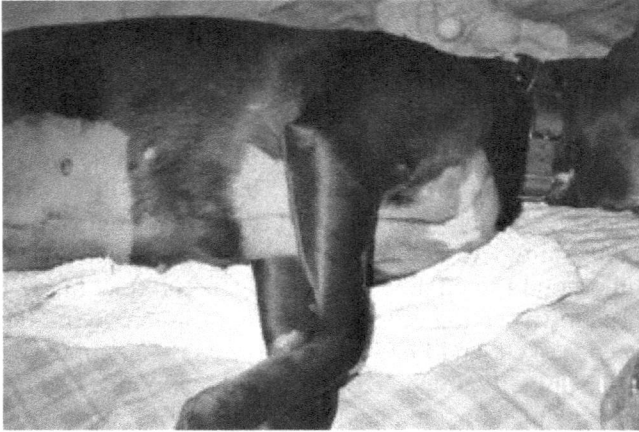

Olivia after her surgery

With this last medical hurdle behind us, I looked forward to enjoying recreational time with Olivia. When the weather cooled, we explored the parks in our neighborhood and walked nearby hiking trails. When it was hot, we would curl up at home on the sofa and just hang out, enjoying each other's company.

But the fear aggression was still an issue. One of my friends, Mike, offered to help. He had a special gift for working with dogs. His longstanding experience at handling dogs and understanding their behavior gave me the confidence to implement his plan. His two adult female labs were healthy, gentle, well-balanced, and well-trained dogs. The younger one, Shelby, was much larger than Olivia. Over a period of several weeks, we would meet in a neutral space that had no territorial significance for any of the dogs, and then he would let Shelby and Olivia, both on leashes, spar with each other for a few seconds before pulling them apart. Shelby's superior size and strength overwhelmed Olivia, and she gradually backed down and stopped initiating attacks. Once Shelby's role as the alpha dog was established, my friend brought both dogs into my house. I stood by his dogs while he took Olivia's leash and gently corrected her as she snarled and growled at the others. After a few sessions of this, Olivia came to tolerate having these other dogs in her space. I don't believe she ever liked it, but that she was able to tolerate it and lay down quietly in their presence was a huge victory! This tolerance extended to other dogs in other situations as well, and Olivia stayed calm as long as they kept a safe distance.

This period with Olivia being physically healthy and strong was unfortunately short lived, lasting only six months or so. Olivia contracted Valley Fever, which is caused by a relatively common fungus indigenous to the deserts in the Southwest. Both people and animals can contract it, though it is not contagious between the two or even between individuals of the same species. Scientifically known as Coccidioidomycosis, its spores reside in the soil, and can survive for a long time in harsh environmental conditions such as heat, cold and drought. When the soil is disturbed, the spores become airborne, are inhaled, and can settle in the lungs. In dogs, the fungus can provoke a host of disorders, including: skin ulcers, abscesses, bone lesions, severe joint pain, heart inflammation, urinary track problems, meningitis, secondary infections and even death. Although all dogs living in the Southwest are likely exposed to this organism, not all manifest the disease. According to a study conducted by the University of Arizona's Valley Fever Center for Excellence, dogs raised from birth in Arizona's Pima or Maricopa counties (the counties where Phoenix and Tucson are located) have a 28% chance of Valley Fever infection by 2 years of age. However, most dogs who test positive for Valley Fever remain asymptomatic, possibly due to having developed an immunity to the disease. The study concluded that on an annual basis, 4% of dogs in Maricopa and Pinal counties will contract Valley Fever and actually show signs of the disease.

Valley Fever is diagnosed using a blood test, called a Cocci test or titer, which measures the amount of antibodies the dog is producing to fight the fungus. The higher the titer reading, the more severe the Valley Fever. The treatment offered by veterinarians is typically Fluconazole, an anti-fungal medication, combined with ongoing monitoring of the dog's immune system to measure if the Valley Fever is still stimulating antibody production. When the treatment is successful, the dog's levels of antibodies naturally decline, indicating that the fungal infection is being eradicated. Otherwise, where the infection is more tenacious as indicated by ongoing high titer levels, continuing treatment is necessary, sometimes for the rest of the dog's life.

After Olivia's Valley Fever diagnosis in 2007, she required extensive on-going care. Her titer reading was 1:265, the highest measurable reading possible on the scale, indicating an extremely severe case. This required the highest dosage possible of the anti-fungal medicine, given twice per day, with on-going tri-monthly monitoring of her titer levels. I added vitamin supplements and probiotics to help strengthen her immune system.

While implementing this aggressive treatment, secondary problems arose, necessitating additional medications. The Valley Fever had attacked her spine, causing a condition called "conscious proprioception," whereby Olivia lost the ability to sense where her feet were, an affliction more common in older dogs with arthritic spines. She also acquired a limp, favoring her back leg. Both of these conditions were treated with the medication Metacam. Other conditions arose from her weakened state, and she soon required Soloxine for hypothyroidism and Proin, to control her urine leakage. The vet suspected she had laryngeal paralysis, causing her to wheeze, requiring me to feed her softer food and experiment with creative ways for her to take her medications.

One approach that was especially effective was to use a mortar and pestle to grind the medications, and then stir them into a warm venison broth. Venison is highly recommended by vets because it is high in protein, low in fat, and less likely to induce allergic reactions. This broth masked the taste of the medications and made the brew more enticing for Olivia. In fact, the warm venison broth seemed to soothe her, as after drinking it, she would curl up on the sofa and fall into a deep sleep, which I believe helped promote her healing.

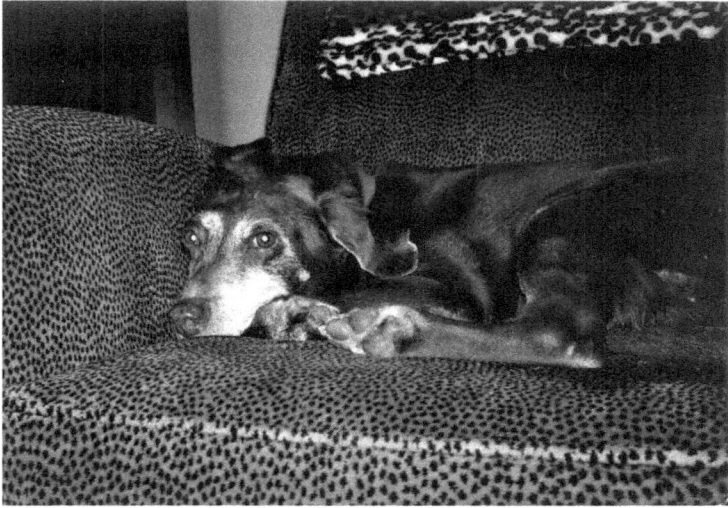

Olivia, November 2008

I now had a very sick dog in a delicate condition that required daily care, lots of medication, a special diet, and ongoing veterinary care to manage her case. Although her needs were extensive, perhaps more than most people would be willing to deal with, I had made a lifetime commitment to her medical care and overall well-being.

A crucial factor in being able to address Olivia's ongoing health challenges was finding the right vet, one who could offer high quality care, open communication and compassion. When I first moved from Atlanta to the Southwest, I researched the local vets, and selected one that appeared reputable and was conveniently located. At first, though the care provided seemed adequate enough, I began to have nagging doubts about my vet selection. In considering my previous visits to him, I remember feeling like he wasn't taking me seriously and my questions were never fully answered. He often kept me waiting, sometimes for over an hour, and during the actual appointment, I got the impression that he was just trying to finish up as quickly as possible. When he interacted with Olivia, she seemed to turn her head away in avoidance. So, I decided to look for a different vet.

I asked my friends for recommendations. A close friend recommended Animal Health Services - a clinic accredited by the AAHA (American Animal Health Association). AAHA is an organization that has developed a set of accreditation standards that are widely used as benchmarks against which to measure excellence in veterinary care. Currently, more than 3,200 veterinary clinics hold the "AAHA-accredited" designation. AAHA developed the accreditation program for many reasons, one of which was to provide a way for animal hospitals to show their excellence to their communities and clients.

I made an appointment with Animal Health Services for an introductory visit to discuss Olivia's health issues. I met with Dr. Faver, the owner of the clinic and one of a team of veterinarians on staff. He reviewed Olivia's medical history, and seemed informed, knowledgeable and up-to-date on current veterinary care issues. He was gentle and compassionate in his interactions with Olivia, and seemed sensitive to her needs. In watching how he interacted with her, and observing how thoroughly he answered my questions, I knew I had chosen well. As it turned out, not only did he provide ongoing high quality care for Olivia, but as her medical complications increased, and my anxiety mounted, he offered me the coaching and emotional support that I needed. I was an emotional wreck, and I was grateful to have found a vet that I could trust.

I followed Dr. Faver's recommendations faithfully, and to my tremendous relief, Olivia's condition greatly improved. Over the course of two and a half years, her titer reading steadily fell, finally fluctuating between 1:4 and 1:16, indicating that the Valley Fever infection was almost purged from her system. I was ecstatic! These results were almost unheard of for dogs with such severe cases of Valley Fever. She was stable, and all the hard work and hours of dedication to treating her had finally paid off.

The disease, however, had taken its toll and seemed to have aged her. The fur around her face and neck had turned grey. She had lost muscle tone and was now somewhat frail. I felt that the Valley Fever had claimed years of her life, years that I had wanted to spend with her, but I couldn't turn back the clock. I continued to treat her secondary conditions - her arthritis, urinary leakage, and lame right leg. But somehow, after conquering the worst of the Valley Fever, by comparison, these seemed very manageable.

We settled into a routine. When I picked up her leash, Olivia would dip into her Labrador stretch, lowering her front paws to the ground and stretching her back paws behind her in anticipation. Then she would raise her head and yawn loudly while wagging her tail vigorously. Olivia loved going to parks and sniffing the bushes. She would hold her nose in the air to savor the aromatic blend of creosote and sage. We would walk the perimeter of a local park, where she would investigate the invisible trails in the grass, and inspect the base of each nearby tree, noting which dogs had preceded her that morning. Deciphering these scents seemed to be akin to me reading the morning newspaper. I was fascinated by her actions, and often wondered what particulars she actually gathered when engrossed in sniffing the outdoors. She had made huge progress at recovering from a variety of medical conditions, and at becoming a well-socialized, sweet dog. I was not looking to get another dog.

Chapter 4: Wednesday, November 3rd, Meeting Harley

On November 3rd, Wednesday morning, Rhonda - a neighbor and good friend - called me somewhat anxiously, asking for my help. She explained that her friend Bill had suddenly and unexpectedly found himself faced with having to find a home for a 140 pound bullmastiff named Harley. Harley had been discovered alone in the apartment where his owner had peacefully died in bed of a heart attack. It was only four days later that an astute neighbor realized something was amiss. When the police arrived, they found Harley by her side, faithfully safeguarding her body. Clearly he had gone for several days without food or water. Since the woman lived by herself, the police were unsure of what to do with Harley. A kindly neighbor and friend of the deceased stepped in and offered to shelter Harley for a day or two until he could get in touch with Bill, the deceased woman's ex-husband.

Years earlier, Bill had accompanied his ex-wife when she selected Harley as a puppy from a breeder. He had helped her pick him out and had grown fond of Harley during his occasional drop-in visits. Now, when the neighbor dropped by both to offer his condolences for his ex-wife's passing, and to hand over Harley's reins, Bill was speechless. However, he took Harley in both out of respect to the memory of his ex-wife and because Harley deserved a good home. He knew full well that he needed to find a different home for Harley, for in his cramped house, he lived with two adult children and their significant others, two grandchildren, and one very aggressive and territorial pit bull. He knew he had to keep the dogs in separate rooms to avert a dog fight.

Firm in his realization that he himself could not keep Harley, the next day Bill called a bullmastiff rescue group for advice. The woman he spoke with instructed him to drop Harley off at a local vet clinic where he could be picked up later. After hanging up, Bill wondered how he would know if Harley was ok and placed in a good home.

That's when Rhonda, while talking to Bill, suggested that I might be able to help. Rhonda knew I had experience in rescuing dogs, and also knew I had a soft spot in my heart for mastiffs. Growing up, our family had a rescued English Mastiff named Coco, so I was familiar with the demands of caring for this unique, colossal breed. Mastiffs were bred more than one hundred years ago to assist English gamekeepers in guarding against poachers. They don't bark very much, and require little exercise or grooming. They were bred to be strong guard dogs, but also to have loyal and gentle, loving temperaments.

Rhonda, hopeful that I might consider rescuing another homeless mastiff, called me immediately. Once she explained the situation, I knew in my heart that I could help and was confident that I could find the best solution for everyone involved. Perhaps Harley could stay with Olivia and me until we placed him in a good home. This arrangement would work only if Harley and Olivia got along with each other. Olivia was older now, and the Valley Fever had made her more docile. With Harley being a male dog, he wouldn't provide any threat to her alpha female status. I immediately called Bill and we agreed to meet later at the mailboxes up the street.

I left my house for the short walk, and as I rounded the corner, a huge bullmastiff appeared that was 140 lbs of solid muscle. His head and neck were as large and round as a basketball, and he immediately brought to mind the image of a linebacker football player with a big head and no neck. His face was covered by a large black mask, made more prominent by his fawn-colored body. His muzzle was broad and deep, solid black, and his face and forehead were covered with wrinkles, much like a Char Pei. His black jowls hung a good two inches below his facial structure and his eyes were caramel brown, keen and alert, with a full four-inch span between them. Clearly he was a purebred from a good breeder and was perhaps two or three years old. He appeared excited to meet me, and carried an air of fearlessness and confidence, tempered by docility. I noted his paws were splayed and seemed to be wider and larger than my hands. His toenails were black and white, long and thick like bird claws. Being more familiar with English Mastiffs, I noted his body proportions differed significantly. As a bullmastiff, he had a broader chest and shorter legs, giving him a much stouter appearance. His cheekbones were set high, leading up to his flat, wrinkled forehead, and his v-shaped ears were held close to the top of his cheeks. Although cute, his ears appeared comically disproportionate to his massive size.

As Harley plodded alongside Bill, the wrinkles in his forehead gave him a permanent frown, but when he opened his mouth, panting with excitement, he appeared to smile at me. Then, I noticed the white star marking on his chest, just as I had seen on Olivia's chest when I first met her seven years ago. Although his was larger and hand-sized, I felt a pang of recognition, and wondered if the similar white star markings held additional significance for the role I would play in rescuing Harley.

Bill and I spoke briefly, then headed back towards my house. Harley – oblivious of his sheer size and strength – pulled Bill along behind him.

"Has he been walked much on a leash?" I asked.

"Well, a little," Bill sighed with resignation. Harley displayed all the mannerisms of a gentle giant. Despite his robust build – big-boned and muscular - he had a very amiable, deliberate demeanor.

Since he outweighed me by a good 10 lbs, I wanted to try walking Harley myself, to see if I could manage him. I felt comfortable trying it since Bill was right there to grab the leash if the situation got out of hand. With Olivia, I had to be cautious walking in public areas, especially in parks, since she had shown so many signs of fear aggression. I hoped this wouldn't be the case with Harley.

Bill handed me the leash, and I was astonished at how different the leash felt connected to Harley. He just wanted to sniff the grass, satisfy his curiosity for nearby scents, and expend some of his rambunctious energy. His pull was much stronger than Olivia's and I knew that if he really wanted to take off, he could easily pull me down the street! After about two minutes, I handed the leash back to Bill.

As we continued walking towards my house, Bill shared with me everything that he knew about Harley - that he was a good dog, that he liked people, and that he was especially good with children.

"He's still a puppy though so he's a bit rambunctious. But he doesn't have a mean bone in his body!" Bill exclaimed.

We finished the short walk down to my house. I had specifically left the back gate unlocked in order to bring Harley into the backyard instead of directly into the house. I wanted to create a more neutral space where Harley and Olivia could meet. With Olivia's history as a bait dog, in spite of the progress we had made, I was still concerned over how she would react to finding a new dog in her territory. By selecting the backyard, perhaps neither dog would feel like they had to protect their territory. The plan was for Bill to stay with Harley in the back while I went inside through the back door to put a leash on Olivia and bring her out into the more neutral meeting area.

Well, it didn't happen that way! As soon as I opened the back patio door and stepped through, in followed Harley – fearlessly curious - dragging Bill unwillingly behind him. I moved quickly to Olivia and stood by the back of the sectional sofa, slipping a leash over her head. Although I kept a tight grip on her leash, it wasn't necessary. To my utter amazement, she got off the sofa, wagged her tail, put her ears back in a sign of friendly submission and allowed Harley to saunter over to greet her. He was so much larger than she was. He slowly extended his head forward and gently sniffed her nose. He panted and began drooling profusely, as is typical of mastiffs when they get excited. Sniffing her all over, he drooled on her back, a long wet clear drool. She didn't seem to mind. Surprisingly, to all appearances they knew each other already, and behaved as though this was a happy reunion! Having satisfied his curiosity in meeting this new dog, Harley settled contentedly on the cool tile floor in front of Olivia. I grabbed some paper towels from the kitchen to try to wipe off some of the drool, but they didn't really absorb it.

Harley drooling

Bill and I walked back out into the yard. I had put grass in two summers ago. It seemed to keep the house cooler in the summer and made it more comfortable for Olivia, as she hated to walk on gravel. She was a Southern girl with delicate paws who loved the feel of grass. She so preferred the grass that before I installed it, she would only relieve herself across the street at the park, even late at night. Now with her health condition, having grass right in the backyard made things much easier for her, and eliminated any possibility of encountering a coyote or javelina in the park after dark.

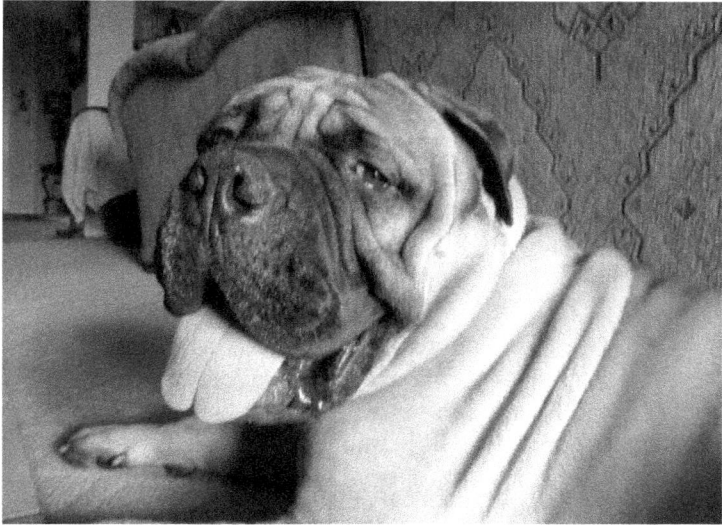

"Let's take Harley back outside for some water," I suggested, in order to put Olivia back on the sofa to rest. I knew that meeting Harley had been exhausting for her. Harley could pant, drool and slobber on the patio and grass all he wanted.

"I'm not sure about keeping Harley on a permanent basis," I told Bill. "I can tell he is a great dog, but I worry he might be too much for Olivia in her frail condition."

I worried that Harley – unaware of his size and strength – might want to play and inadvertently injure Olivia in the process. Dr. Faver had suggested that I treat Olivia the way I would a ninety-year old grandmother.

"But I could keep him until we find a good home for him," I said, understanding that Bill had done his part and couldn't manage Harley any longer.

Bill, visibly relieved, thanked me and said he would check in with me later that evening.

After Bill left, I went to my laundry room to retrieve some cotton rags to use as drool cloths. I put a couple in each room, and went back to the family room where Olivia lay resting. I patted her soft brown head and reassured her that everything would be all right and that we would find Harley a good home. I went out back and gave Harley some food, a Venison bone, and fresh water.

With Harley contentedly gnawing on the bone, I went inside to return Rhonda's calls. She had left three messages and was anxious and excited to know if I was going to keep Harley.

"Well, what do you think?" Rhonda blurted out with excitement.

"Frankly, I'm not sure," I said. "It doesn't seem like he's leash trained, plus he's big and rambunctious. I think he may overwhelm Olivia. I don't want him to knock her over by accident and break one of her bones."

"Yes," Rhonda added. "Those are legitimate concerns." She understood that Harley would be too much for me to take on, especially given my other responsibilities helping to care for my parents.

Wednesday Afternoon

With Harley settled out back, I proceeded to develop a plan of action to find Harley a good home. I put together a list of local rescue organizations to contact and began the layout of a flyer describing Harley. Rhonda volunteered her assistance. She sent her daughter Sarah over to take some photographs of Harley for the flyers. Sarah really captured the essence of Harley's gentle spirit and his immense size. Soon we were calling, emailing, and texting info out about Harley. I knew that the faster we could spread the word the faster we could get Harley into the home he deserved. I was confident we would be able to find him a good home. In the meantime, I called my parents to tell them the news. My father was thrilled that I had stepped in to help in this situation.

"I'll be right over," he said.

My father and I both loved really big dogs, and we were passionate about helping dogs in need. While my mother loved big dogs too, Olivia came first, and as far as she was concerned, my dog was their dog, and one dog was enough. She knew that Olivia had been very sick and knew that I needed to focus my energy and financial resources on taking care of her.

Harley smiling after meeting Olivia

The doorbell rang. My father smiled as he walked in and saw Harley at the back patio door. He greeted Olivia with a pat on her head and she wagged her tail in response. He then proceeded to the back patio to meet Harley.

"He's a big guy!" my father declared. "Your mother didn't come because she didn't want to be tempted into adopting a dog this size."

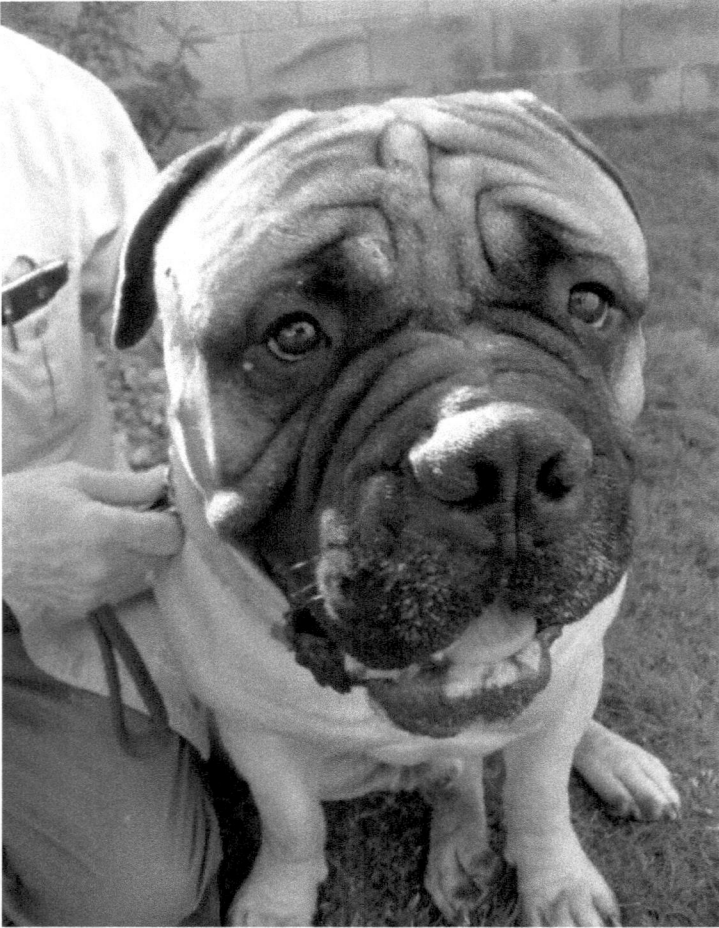

"He's a big guy!"

I understood immediately what he meant. Our whole family had a soft spot for dogs, and my mother knew if she saw Harley, she would fall in love and want to adopt him. That was not a option, however, as my parents were in their mid 70's and were struggling with medical conditions – she with failing eyesight and he with a heart condition.

As soon as Harley saw my father through the glass door, there was an instant connection. Harley wagged his tail and grinned broadly as he lifted his front legs in anticipation. Their mutual greetings were so warmly given and received, a casual observer would have sworn he was seeing a happy reunion. We sat on the patio outside while I told my father how the day transpired, and what I knew of Harley's history. Olivia remained inside on the sofa, comfortably sleeping, content in the moment.

Harley and my father getting to know each other

While my father played with Harley in the backyard, I called my brother, who had recently rescued a homeless English Mastiff named Icon. I knew he would be interested in learning about Harley. He listened as I shared with him what had happened, and not surprisingly, he suggested that I adopt him. For the previous two years, my brother had been encouraging me to adopt an English Mastiff as company for Olivia, and as a guard dog for me. Olivia had never really displayed guard dog traits. She was a companion dog and I loved her for that. But now the issue arose again.

"Think about it," my brother said. "Mastiffs are great guard dogs. You live alone and if someone tried to break in, Harley would protect you! These opportunities don't come along all that often."

Although I did consider keeping him, I felt the timing was all wrong. I needed instead to focus all my energy on getting Harley properly placed.

Later that evening Bill called back to check in. I told him Harley was doing well and would spend the night with me. At this point, based on my past experience of placing rescue dogs, I felt very comfortable with him, and was confident that we would soon find the right match.

Wednesday Evening

As darkness fell upon us, my father took Harley inside to visit with Olivia again. He had calmed down quite a bit since his arrival early that afternoon, having been fed, and having received lots of attention throughout the afternoon – from Sarah, my father, and me. My father had gone out earlier to buy food and supplies that Harley needed, even for such a short stay – dog food and a chain choke collar to better control him while he adjusted to us. Now my father calmly sat with Harley on one side of the sofa, and Olivia and I on the other. We remained there relaxed with both dogs looking at each other. Both were content and peaceful. After a few minutes, Olivia lay her head down, closed her eyes and fell asleep. Harley did the same. It was astonishing to see that both seemed to have accepted each other so quickly.

Best friends

Both my father and I felt that Olivia and Harley would be able to stay together in the same house as long as we kept them somewhat separated and kept an eye on them. I placed a large crate on the back patio for Harley so he would have a secure den for the night. There were several warm blankets inside the crate, and I left the crate door open so he could go in and out freely during the night. At this time of year, the daytime in the Southwest was hot, but the desert nights cooled off considerably. I knew Harley would be fine spending the night outside.

With both dogs comfortably settled in for the evening, my father left for home, and I returned to work on the flyer. As I worked on it, Harley stared at me through the sliding glass door, tilting his head to the left and right, as if to ask me what I was doing. He clearly was not interested in retiring to his crate, but instead rapped on the glass patio door with his paw. Knowing that he was well-fed and had a comfortable den to sleep in, I continued working on the flyer, hoping that Harley would soon tire of watching me and go to sleep.

November 3, 2010

Hi,

My name is Harley. I am a purebred bullmastiff (my former owner's friends can't find my papers, but I am from a breeder in Texas, we don't know who the breeder is, or how to locate them). Four days ago, my owner, a female middle-aged woman died of a massive heart attack, on October 30, 2010. Right now, I am looking for a safe, loving, permanent home. I am almost 2 years old and love people and children. I have an excellent temperament, wag my tail, and love affection. I have been around small children, and like other dogs, but still need some training on how to remain calm. I also need a little leash training but I am really willing to learn and please. I would also love a big fenced yard to play in.

Right now I weigh between 130 -150 lbs. My neck size is 28 inches and I am about 28" floor to shoulder height. I am also about 42" from nose to butt (not tail). My color is true fawn with a black face. I am not neutered.

I need love and a special home. Please email this to anyone you think may want to adopt me.

Contact Rose
Home: xxxxxxxx
Cell: xxxxxxxxx
Email: xxxxxxxxxxxxxxxxxx

After completing the flyer, I gave Olivia her evening medicine, made sure she was tucked in, and turned the lights out in the family room. I entered the master bedroom and turned the light on.

Harley immediately started pawing at the glass door, so I quickly shut the lights off. I had forgotten the drapes were still open, so Harley could see me through the master bedroom sliding glass door that led to the back patio. He continued to paw at the glass door and I could feel him staring at me, imploring me to let him in. My heart melted. I shut the bedroom door to block entrance into the family room where Olivia was, and I opened the sliding glass door for Harley. He was ecstatic. He ran in and, like a horse preparing to leap over a hurdle, he backed up and launched himself up onto my bed. He quickly identified my side and dropped his massive frame there. As fond of Harley as I was, I had my limits! With a few treats, I coaxed him to the other side of the bed, and had him lay on a cover sheet, knowing he would probably drool in his sleep. Now Harley was content. The ritual seemed quite familiar to him, so I surmised that he must have slept in bed with his previous owner.

"Okay," I thought to myself, "I will let him stay. If Olivia needs me during the night she'll just bark outside the master bedroom door."

Harley settled in bed for the night

53

Harley and I settled into bed together. He quickly calmed down and fell asleep by my side. I was confident that we would find the right match and so planned on continuing the search for Harley's permanent home in the morning.

Chapter 5: Thursday, November 4th, The Adoption

The next morning, I woke to an unusual grunting sound. I opened my eyes and saw Harley sitting beside my bed, staring at me, his large caramel eyes level with mine. He grunted again softly, like a muted pig snorting, telling me that it was time to get up. I was exhausted, having slept poorly. Harley had arisen numerous times during the night, restlessly wanting to explore and re-explore his new environment. Every time he jumped on or off the bed, I awoke startled. Now, acceding to Harley, I stepped out of the bed and opened the screen door to let him outside while I went to check on Olivia. She wagged her tail when she saw me, alert and ready for her morning walk. I kept Harley in the backyard, and took Olivia out the front door to make a quick visit to her favorite nearby park. I wanted to tire her out with a short walk so she would be calmer around Harley, minimizing the potential for any surfacing of her fear aggression. Harley watched us intently as I closed and locked the front door.

As we left the vicinity of the house and headed up the street to the park, he tried to follow us along the fence of the backyard, letting out an enormous howl. The farther we progressed from the house, the louder the howls became, each filled with despondence and anguish over being left behind. The howling continued as we walked around the park, getting louder and more desperate, pleading with us to return. We hurriedly finished our walk around the park and headed home. As soon as Harley heard us approaching, he quieted down.

Once we were back inside the house, he wagged his tail, smiling, infinitely relieved to have us back. "Classic symptoms of separation anxiety," I said to myself with dismay, knowing it might make it harder to find the right match for him. Separation anxiety is a condition that typically manifests in one of two ways. The first is continual howling, barking or crying. The second is enacting various degrees of destruction to the home, crate, yard or environment in which they are left. Harley displayed both. In addition to howling, I noticed from the drool and paw prints that he had been jumping on the sliding glass door while we were out on our walk. Outside, I saw that Harley had vomited part of the venison bone as well.

But his gentle disposition and the uniqueness of his breed were true assets, so much so that in the back of my mind, I was still considering whether or not I could keep him myself. But with Olivia's health issues, I just couldn't manage taking care of both of them.

Mid-morning, my parents came over. My mother, unable to resist any longer, had accompanied my father to meet Harley. As they came in and my mother sat down in her favorite chair, Harley sauntered over to sit next to her, staring adoringly into her eyes. He waited expectantly, wagging his tail. As she petted his head, he closed his eyes and broke into a broad grin.

"Rose," my mother commented to me, "much as I hate to say it, he really is beautiful and seems very content here. You know, we would take him if we could, but at our age, he's just too big of a dog for us to take care of. Are you sure you don't want to keep him? He seems so gentle and loving."

Harley and my mother

"I wish I could, but it's more than I can take on right now," I said. "And with Olivia being so fragile, and he so full

56

of energy, I'm worried he'll unintentionally knock Olivia over!"

My mother nodded in agreement. We continued chatting about Harley and the rescue process.

After my parents left, I returned to my study to see if I had any responses to the emails I had sent out on Wednesday. To my surprise, my in-box was already flooded with responses. People loved both the picture of Harley on the flyer, and his description. Clearly, to these people, Harley was extremely special, and they were responding!

One of the emails was from Dawn, the regional coordinator of the American Bullmastiff Association Rescue Service (ABARAS). I had been planning on contacting her, knowing that the mastiff rescue groups could play an instrumental role in finding a home for Harley. They would recognize how exemplary he was of his breed, and they would be well informed about the breed characteristics and what's involved in caring for such a large dog. Dawn informed me that she had a colleague named Troy who might be interested in taking Harley. Troy had had two other bullmastiffs in the past – one which had died of cancer many years earlier and the other which had fallen victim to the melamine atrocity perpetrated by several overseas raw material suppliers for dog food. He had a large house that was newly renovated, a spacious yard, a good job as a police officer, and most importantly, he was experienced and familiar with the breed. He sounded like an ideal match. I replied to Dawn asking her to have Troy call me.

I stepped outside to enjoy the luminous desert sunset and the cool evening air. Harley followed me, staying close by my side, and Olivia trailed soon after. We stood in the backyard, relishing the privacy afforded by the thicket of bushes and scattered cacti in the wash through the view fencing. Suddenly, Harley perked his ears up and stared into the distance. I followed his gaze to what appeared to be an adult coyote, watching us intently through the bars of the fence. Harley instinctively moved forward, placing himself between the coyote and Olivia and me. Perhaps deterred by his sheer size, the coyote hesitated, then turned and fled into the hills. I had heard stories of coyotes jumping 6 ft fences and attacking smaller dogs or cats. I took a deep breath and shuttled Olivia inside. Harley patrolled the perimeter, sniffing for any further signs of the coyote. Then, satisfied that the grounds were secure, he joined us inside.

That evening, Troy called me from a restaurant where he was out dining with friends. We kept our conversation brief so he could return to his gathering. He mentioned that both of his previous bullmastiffs had also been rescue dogs. Being single, he had time to spend with Harley, training and exercising him, and had already made provisions for adopting a large dog. For example, he had put in an extra-large doggie door, one large enough to accommodate a bullmastiff. He had a large fenced-in backyard. In terms of knowledge and experience, he knew how to train and care for this breed. Financially, he seemed to have the necessary resources to cover food and veterinary care.

In response to my description of Harley, Troy said he was interested in coming out to meet him. I invited him to visit, and offered to send him directions if he emailed me when he returned home. As soon as I hung up the phone, I called Bill to let him know that we had found a prospective home. Relieved, with Olivia sleeping in the family room and Harley resting comfortably on my bed, we all settled in for the night.

Chapter 6: Friday, November 5th, The Match

The next morning, I once again woke up to a soft snort and the intent gaze of large caramel eyes inches from my face. Like the previous night, I had slept fitfully, waking each time Harley restlessly jumped on or off the bed throughout the night. Although I have a sturdy, king-sized iron-framed bed that easily supported his weight, 140 pounds launching off or landing on the mattress invariably jolted me awake. Harley slept in one of two positions. The first was resting his head on a pillow, stretched out lengthwise like a person, keeping an eye on me while I drifted off to sleep. The other added to my sleep disruptions. Harley had discovered the oak night stand beside my bed was just the right height and size for him to rest his head on. It was an oddly comical position – sleeping sideways on the bed, his rear pressing against me while his head lay on the stand. The problem was that it was an antique I had inherited from my grandmother, and with its age, came squeaking whenever weight was applied to it. So, between the table squeaking and the bed shuddering, I was so exhausted in the morning that I implored for ten more minutes of rest, but Harley "harrumphed" and lifted his front legs so insistently that I reluctantly arose.

I let Harley out into the backyard, and approached him with a large bowl of kibble. Upon seeing his dog dish, he started drooling, leaving little puddles around his feet. I then prepared Olivia's medications and gave her both the food and medications. Once fed, I took Olivia for a brief walk. We walked briskly, and like the day before, Harley howled the moment we were out of his sight. Although I really wanted to bring Harley, he wasn't leash trained, and I wasn't sure I could manage walking both him and Olivia at the same time.

When we returned, I checked my emails to see if Troy had followed up. There were many responses and inquiries about Harley, but none from Troy. I proceeded with my chores and activities for the day.

Several hours passed, and by late morning, I still hadn't received an email from Troy. Perhaps he had changed his mind. I picked up the phone and called him.

"Hi Troy, are you still interested in coming out to meet Harley?" I asked.

Troy replied, "Yes, definitely. I just hadn't gotten around to emailing you yet."

"Well," I replied, "if you are serious about considering him for adoption, I'd appreciate it if you could come today. I have my hands full with taking care of two dogs."

"I'll be there around one," he promised.

Troy was driving up from the outskirts of the city, a good two-hour drive away. In the interim, I called Bill to let him know that Troy was coming to my house that afternoon. To my surprise, Bill insisted he be there to meet Troy. I then called my parents to give them an update on the situation, and they too insisted on being there to meet Troy. Although neither Bill nor my parents were able to adopt Harley, they had nonetheless bonded with him and considered him part of their family. In some ways I felt like a chaperone for the first meeting of an arranged marriage, where all the relatives gather to approve the suitor.

As one o'clock approached, one by one people started coming over. Olivia lay in her bed watching the activity, resting with her head on her paws, her eyes open and alert. My parents arrived first. My father went outside to the back patio to sit with Harley. My mother remained in the family room to chat with me while I finished doing the dishes. Bill soon followed and joined my father out back with Harley.

Troy finally arrived, pulling up in a large SUV, accompanied by his girlfriend. Upon hearing the doorbell, I opened the door and to my amazement, the man before me resembled a bullmastiff! Troy was tall, in his mid-thirties, thickset with a broad neck - very muscular, perhaps from lifting weights in his spare time. He exuded confidence, strength and determination. His girlfriend was tall and slim, with long dark brown curly hair.

"He seems like the perfect match for Harley," I thought to myself. I invited them in and after introductions to my father and Bill, guided everyone out to the patio where Troy could meet Harley. He had come prepared with a leash and some dog treats.

"He's a good looking bullmastiff!" Troy exclaimed.

Harley meeting his new owner

We sat down around the patio. Harley sat next to Troy, giving him his paw in a friendly greeting, wagging his tail. Troy pulled out the treats and gave Harley a few commands, assessing Harley's level of training and obedience.

At that moment, my mother, who had been inside patting Olivia, joined us outside. After exchanging greetings with Troy and his girlfriend, she politely asked if she could see his badge, much like a future mother-in-law might do to verify a suitor's credentials. Troy showed her his badge, and she nodded her approval. We continued to talk. Troy described what Harley's living environment would be like, offering that he had a large house, a large doggie door suitable for Harley, and a yard that was about three times the size of mine.

Troy patiently answered our questions, letting us size him up to see if he would be the right match. Troy told us about his previous bullmastiffs. He clearly was very knowledgeable about the breed, and had the physical strength to train and care for a large dog. He then asked questions about Harley. Bill explained that Harley was about two or three years old, and had come from a bullmastiff breeder. Bill's ex-wife had raised him from the time he was six weeks old.

Finally, when Troy asked if we had any concerns, I told him about Harley's separation anxiety. Troy shrugged it off, explaining that he was currently recovering from recent back surgery, and was going to be home a lot during the recuperation period. This would, he explained, give him time to work with Harley, and help him get acclimated to his new home. As part of his recovery, his doctor wanted him to walk two miles per day, which he planned to do with Harley, so he could include leash training as well. With this last hurdle overcome, the match seemed ideal. By the end of the meeting, everyone was confident that Harley would be well taken care of.

Having secured our approval, Troy put the leash on Harley, and took him out the back pathway to his vehicle. As we parted, Troy promised that we could come see Harley anytime we wanted. Knowing from experience that sometimes even the best of matches can go wrong, I asked Troy to contact me if things didn't work out.

Harley jumped into the back of the SUV. I gave Troy the leftover dog food, and handed him Harley's drool cloth. Harley wagged his tail as we kissed him and hugged him goodbye. As they drove off, I felt empty inside. The backyard seemed strangely unfamiliar and uninviting now.

Chapter 7: Saturday November 6th, Remorse

The next morning, I awoke well-rested and refreshed, having slept soundly throughout the night. As I glanced at the clock, I realized I'd slept longer than I had intended. Then it struck me – Harley was gone. The snorting, grunting, the pool of brown eyes, the rearing up on his hind legs – these were all missing. The house seemed empty and quiet without him.

As I prepared Olivia's breakfast and medications, she seemed to miss him too. She scouted around the house, sniffing as she went, pausing at places where Harley used to rest. As I reflected on Harley, I considered the other dozen or so rescue dogs I had re-homed. I was relieved that I had found a good match for Harley, and was confident in Troy's ability to care for him. Yet, I felt a sense of loss when Troy drove away with Harley. The image of Harley watching us from the back window of the SUV, grinning broadly and drooling, resurfaced in my mind with a pang of regret. I was surprised at these feelings. In the past, when I successfully placed a dog, I would feel a great sense of relief and satisfaction, allowing me to emotionally move on to my next project. This case was closed. Harley was in a really good home. That I missed his smiling, gentle gaze as he deferentially followed me around the house, drooling where we settled, was no longer relevant.

I spent the rest of day responding to the barrage of emails and phone calls I'd received in response to Harley's flyer. So many organizations had forwarded information about Harley to other people and organizations that it had reached a critical mass. Frankly, I was stunned at the response. People from around the country shared heartwarming stories of the lives of their bullmastiff's and the loss they experienced when their companions passed. Then, from seeing Harley's photograph and reading his description in the flyer, they made a decision to once again open their hearts and home to an unknown bullmastiff in need. I was amazed at how this one rescue dog could have such a profound impact on so many people.

Chapter 8: Sunday November 7th, Peaceful Places

The next morning, I poured myself a cup of coffee and sat out on the back patio with Olivia. The air was cool and crisp and I savored the quietude while I watched Olivia. She walked across the patio sniffing, then stepped onto the grass, her nose following the pathway across the yard to the back. I watched as she sniffed the grass and bushes. Was it my imagination or was she still looking for Harley? Olivia did seem to connect with Harley, an unimaginable milestone given her history as a bait dog. She really did seem to miss him.

To take our minds off Harley, I decided a long walk was in order. I snapped the leash onto Olivia's collar and off we went, falling into a familiar stride, neither pulling the other, the leash more a physical manifestation of the deep connection we felt. We were happy. We were in a peaceful place.

Chapter 9: Monday November 8th, The Check-in

Two days had passed since Troy had adopted Harley, and I hadn't heard anything since. I was somewhat surprised, as I always ask new owners to email or call to let me know how things are going. Unable to wait any longer, later that afternoon I called Troy and left him a message. He called back a few hours later.

"Sorry I missed your call. I was putting up shelves in the garage with a friend."

"How's Harley doing?" I asked.

Troy hesitated. "You know, Harley's been showing signs of separation anxiety. Rose, I know you had mentioned earlier that he had some separation anxiety, but how bad was it?"

"Not bad really," I said. "But, to be honest with you, I rarely left him alone. The only times I left him alone were when I took Olivia to the park and left him in the backyard. He did howl but calmed down after we returned."

"Well," Troy said, "I've been walking him twice a day about two and a half miles each time. I'm guessing this regular exercise will temper his anxiety and help him to adjust to his new home."

I agreed and we spoke for a few more minutes. Troy had been working with Harley on basic commands and walking without pulling at the leash – both of which were going very well. He mentioned that he was still trying to get a hold of Dawn from the American Bullmastiff Association Rescue Service (ABARS) because Harley, as a rescue dog, qualified for a discount on veterinary services.

I felt reassured after talking with Troy. With the exception of the separation anxiety, it sounded like all was well, and Harley and Troy were getting along fine. From my experience in working with rescue dogs, particularly with those who had been traumatized, the bonding process can be delayed. I was relieved that this did not seem to be the case with Harley and Troy.

Chapter 10: Tuesday November 9th, A Change of Pace

Today was my father's birthday. With Harley successfully placed, and Olivia's health stabilized, we wanted to do something really special to celebrate. I felt we needed to shift our focus from dogs back to people, and I found myself looking forward to spending time with my parents. My mother suggested we drive north to Prescott for lunch. It was a beautiful fall morning, albeit warm, and Prescott offered a cooler climate with crisp breezes and pine forests. We had a pleasant lunch there, but despite our best intentions, soon found ourselves conversing about Harley again. We talked about his separation anxiety. Harley had been alone in the apartment with his deceased owner for four days, probably without food or water. The mastiff breed is known for being extremely loyal and devoted to their owners. Did Harley have any understanding of what had happened? I'd read countless stories over the years of dogs that would not leave their owner's grave. I wondered if Harley understood that his owner had died, and that his three-day stint with Olivia and me was just until we could get him into a permanent home. I confided to my parents that I still missed Harley, and to my fond amusement, they admitted they felt the same way.

When we got returned home, Olivia greeted us from the Lazy Boy chair she loved to sleep in. She wagged her tail and, as we all plopped down on various pieces of furniture, Olivia stepped out back and barked as usual, announcing the safe return of her pack.

That evening, I reflected back on my telephone conversation with Troy, and replayed him mentioning Harley's separation anxiety. The tone in his voice when he said it hinted that it may have been more serious than he let on. I wondered if Harley had been left alone and chewed or dug up something. Big mastiffs can do a lot of damage in a short amount of time. I slept fitfully that night with Harley on my mind.

Chapter 11: Wednesday November 10ᵗʰ, What if....

Ever since my conversation with Troy on Monday evening, I couldn't get Harley out of my thoughts. I wondered if I had made the right decision. Troy's words echoed again in my mind. "He's been showing signs of separation anxiety." Would Troy be able to deal with this? Could Harley overcome his fears of being alone? I started doubting myself, wondering whether I should have found a way to care for Harley myself.

I ran through the decision-making process in my mind once again. Had I the time and energy to take on another dog, particularly a rescue dog that may need additional attention? Had I the financial resources to cover the lifetime food and health expenses for a dog of this size? When I rescued Olivia, I never imagined how many health issues would develop. Given Harley's size, did I have a high degree of confidence that I could have trained him, and physically handled walking two dogs – one of which outweighed me? The more I considered these questions, the more I concluded my answers hadn't changed.

"Stop second guessing what was right," I told myself. Troy had already given a home to two previous bullmastiffs, and since they passed on, he had been in constant contact with the American Bullmastiff Association Rescue Service, looking for another rescue dog in need. He had a home with a backyard at least three times the size of mine. He had renovated his house to accommodate a large dog - including adding a large doggie door and laying down tile throughout. Troy clearly loved dogs, and had the financial resources to cover vet and food expenses. He came highly recommended by the American Bullmastiff Association Rescue Service. What more could I ask for? But I still missed Harley, and it seemed like Olivia did too – she continued looking for him.

Chapter 12: Thursday November 11th, In Retrospect

Looking back on this day now, I realize that Olivia's condition was worsening. On that morning when we went for our daily walk, Olivia seemed to walk a bit slower than usual, and her breathing became labored halfway through our normal route. I kept glancing at her, realizing that something didn't seem quite right. I could see her ribcage expand and contract as she barked at other dogs along the walk. With our slowed pace, the walk took us almost twice as long as usual. When we returned home, she climbed onto her spot on the sofa and lay down to rest while I readied myself to leave for a seminar. As I changed my clothes, I considered that perhaps the new batch of venison broth I prepared may have been too rich for her. I decided to drop her off at my parent's house so that they could keep an eye on her while I was out.

When I returned from the seminar, my mother looked concerned.

"What's wrong?" I asked.

"Olivia's lethargic and not acting herself," my mother said. "When I came back in the house from being out earlier, Olivia didn't even raise her head."

My mother always felt strongly connected with Olivia, and had been the one who first recognized that Olivia was sick with Valley Fever over two years ago. Now with my mother worried that something was amiss, I trembled inside, but tried not to overreact.

"Maybe our walk was too long this morning," I said, unconvincing even to myself. "She is getting older and I should probably shorten our walks a bit."

My mother shook her head. "Her stomach seems bloated. She's been drinking a lot but hasn't eaten anything." Olivia looked up at me and dropped her head on the pillow. I could tell she was tired and not feeling well.

"I'll take her home and watch her this evening," I told my mother.

After returning home, I fixed her a small snack, and then sat on the sofa beside her to stroke her fur while I relaxed after my long day. She snuggled against me and fell soundly asleep.

Chapter 13: Friday November 12th, The Crisis

The next morning when I awoke, my first thought was of Olivia. She had slept soundly through the night, not waking when I arose at various times to check on her. Now, her eyes were open and her tail quivered in a morning greeting. I went into the kitchen and after a few minutes, she got off the sofa and joined me. Her gait was unsteady and lethargic so I decided to skip our usual morning walk. Instead, I prepared and gave her medications and food, which to my relief, she devoured hungrily. Afterwards, she retired to the sofa to rest. Judging by her lack of energy, she was definitely not her usual self.

Uncertain what my next step should be, I phoned my parents to let them know that Olivia's condition had worsened, and to discuss our options. We all agreed that her condition seemed serious enough to warrant a return visit to the vet.

I called Animal Health Services, and learned that my regular vet, Dr. Faver, was out of town until Tuesday, but if I hurried I could get in to see Dr. DeKing at 10:00 AM that day. I was dismayed that Dr. Faver wasn't available, as both Olivia and I really liked him. For the past two years, he had helped us through so many medical hurdles with the Valley Fever and its complications, and while I wasn't really comfortable seeing a new vet, Olivia needed help now. On the drive there, Olivia sat quietly in the back seat while I spoke to her reassuringly.

At Animal Health Services, I pulled into a spot close to the entrance to accommodate Olivia's weakened state. I gently helped her out of the car. As we approached the door, Olivia suddenly squatted and defecated. The fecal matter was unusually dark. I checked in with the receptionist, and let her know what had just happened, including the unusual color of the feces. She promptly went outside to retrieve a sample and brought it back for testing. Everyone at Animal Health Services was thorough and helpful, and made us feel that we were in good hands.

Prior to the exam, an assistant weighed Olivia and found she was 2 pounds heavier than her normal weight, likely due to bloating with excess fluids. In the exam room, the veterinary assistant Erin came in and greeted us. Erin was a cheerful young redhead in her early 20's with blue eyes, a quick smile, and a clear love for all animals. She checked all of Olivia's vital signs including temperature, gums and pulse, and took note of Olivia's symptoms.

When Dr. DeKing walked into the room, my heart sank. She seemed quite young, too young in my mind to be an experienced veterinarian. Given that I had had so many bad experiences with vets in the past, my first instinct was to mistrust her. But though I had standing appointments with Dr. Faver every six weeks, and the next one was only four days away, Olivia was clearly sick and needed immediate attention. "Here we go again, one more hurdle, one more vet. Hopefully we can get Olivia feeling better, and then come back on Tuesday for a recheck with Dr. Faver," I conceded.

Olivia and I were quiet as the vet examined her.

"What's been going on?" she asked.

I reviewed the details of what I had observed, and then took a deep breath.

"We tested her stool and did find blood in it," she said.

I thought to myself that this was not a good sign.

"I'd like to do a complete blood profile on her, and an ultrasound. Do you have an hour or so to wait?" She asked.

"Of course," I replied. I knew these tests were a necessary part of the diagnosis. As we waited in the exam room, the minutes seemed like hours. Yet, I was confident that we would get through this, just as we had countless times before.

Finally, Dr. DeKing returned and asked me to step across the hall to her office to discuss the test results. Dr. Faver had done this with us before on several occasions when he had unsettling news, often accompanied by an X-ray or ultrasound results. I felt adrenaline rush through my body as I prepared for bad news. Dr. DeKing had found that Olivia's albumin levels were very low, perhaps indicating stomach or intestinal ulcerations. She asked to keep Olivia for the day for observation and administration of fluids. I agreed and kissed Olivia goodbye, telling her I would be back at the end of the day. Olivia flattened her ears back and looked away, as if to say "I can't believe we have to go through this again." I suspect she really did understand what I said because, heaven knows, we'd been through this before.

I exited the clinic, feeling tightness in the pit of my stomach as I started the forty minute drive back home. Just when I thought Olivia was well on her way to recovery, she had taken a sudden turn for the worse. I was very concerned. Dr. Faver had warned me that sometimes with older dogs, things can go downhill very quickly. His advice confused me at the time, because I had thought Olivia was only seven, still young with many years ahead of her. But Dr. Faver had suspected the rescue group had misjudged her age. He placed her closer to twelve, though we agreed that the Valley Fever and its complications may have greatly accelerated the aging process.

In the late afternoon, I returned to the vet, with my father accompanying me for moral support. When Olivia saw me in the exam room, she wagged her tail happily with considerable relief.

Dr. DeKing reviewed with us all the blood work and ultrasound test results. She said that Olivia's albumin levels were really low, which could indicate a tumor in her intestinal tract. Olivia also had blood in her stool, which could indicate that the tumor was ulcerated and bleeding. If she were to bleed profusely, surgery would be required – a high risk for a dog of Olivia's age. The clinic had conducted an ultrasound to try to locate a possible tumor, but the results were inconclusive. Dr. DeKing indicated that the stool blood could also be a sign of bleeding from another organ. Without exploratory surgery, it simply wasn't possible to know. Alternatively, Dr. DeKing suggested we could try a regimen of medications to stabilize her for the weekend, or at least until Dr. Faver returned. I chose the latter. I knew I didn't want Olivia to go through the trauma of major surgery. She just couldn't take any more. Between her age and the effects of the Valley Fever, I knew it would be very difficult for her to recover from any type of surgery.

In concluding the meeting, Erin reviewed the medication list with me, dividing out which needed to be administered with food, and which without. Finally, as we left the vet's office, I couldn't help but smile sadly as I watched poor Olivia scurrying out the door as quickly as her feeble legs would carry her, making a beeline for our car before anyone changed their mind.

Since Animal Health Services would be closed over the weekend, I needed to have a backup plan in case Olivia's condition worsened. The nearest emergency vet was almost an hour away. Dr. DeKing had warned me that if the ulceration did rupture, I would only have an hour or two to get Olivia into emergency surgery. I didn't want to consider it, but the last option for Olivia's condition was euthanasia.

"No," I thought to myself. "Olivia and I have beaten so many medical problems over the years. We can conquer this one, too."

On the way home, I sat in the back seat with Olivia while my father drove. I stroked her head and spoke comfortingly to her during the ride. When we arrived at my parents' house, I rolled the window down so my mother could greet her and kiss her on the forehead.

Once back home, I fed Olivia and gave her the recommended medications. Her appetite was satisfactory and I felt hopeful. She seemed relaxed and happy to be back at home resting on her favorite spot on the sofa. With Olivia settled in, I decided to check my emails and respond to the inquiries that continued to stream in about Harley.

I saw that Troy had sent me an email titled "Regarding big mastiff." I opened it and the email read as follows:

Hi Rose,

Just wanted to email you since I couldn't find your phone number. You asked me to let you know if I encountered any problems during the settling-in process. I wanted to let you know that I have. I'm not sure what Harley's prior living situation was like, but he really has an extreme case of separation anxiety. He already ruined an interior room door from scratching and biting, and he starts scratching at the front door as soon as I walk out the door to leave. He actually broke out of his metal dog crate and refuses to stay in it when I leave. I'm afraid when I start work this week, and will be gone for 10 or more hours a day, he may damage even more things. I just put an extreme amount of time and money into my house and I don't want him to ruin it. I couldn't get in touch with Dawn, so I went ahead and got him neutered and had his shots updated, which was quite a financial investment.

I'm not sure what to do since he does this whenever he is left completely alone. To be honest, maybe I was spoiled by having such well behaved dogs prior to him. He is a very good dog, but needs constant attention. When I return to work, I won't be able to give him this attention, and he may act out, which is not really his fault. Please let me know what you think about this situation, as I promised you I would let you know if there was a problem. Since I don't have your number, you can call me if you like.

Troy

Alarmed by his email, I immediately returned to the family room to call Troy. He explained in detail some of the damage Harley had done. Harley had scratched at the doors and ripped out the door frames. He had peed on the couch. He'd even torn apart his metal dog crate. While Troy and I discussed the situation with Harley, Olivia sat and watched me attentively. She looked straight into my eyes and perked her ears up every time she heard Harley's name.

"Do you miss him?" Troy asked.

"Yes," I said knowing that I was speaking not only for myself but for Olivia, and my parents, too.

"Do you want him back?" Troy asked.

A flood of emotions welled up inside and staggered me. The past 10 days flashed through my mind with startling clarity. Harley standing guard over his deceased owner. His unexpected bonding with Olivia. Waking up to an anxious grunt, his warm breath flowing over my face as he lifted his legs in joyous relief to my waking. Fending off a coyote intruder, protecting both Olivia and me as his family. The irony struck me – this big, fierce protector was deathly afraid of being alone. He needed someone to protect, someone who needed his massive size and strength, someone he could watch over with every fiber of his being. He needed to be needed.

"Rose, are you there?" he asked, breaking into my thoughts.

"Yes," I said, returning to the moment. "I'm still here. And..." I hesitated. "Yes, I want Harley back."

There, it was done. My decision was made. After I hung up, I waited for remorse, regret, anything to suggest that I hadn't really meant it, that I fully intended to start the search anew for yet another home and owner for Harley. None came. Harley was coming home – to me.

We arranged to make the exchange on Sunday, now two days away, at a location about halfway between us at a Cabela's Outfitter Store. I had been to Cabela's before. It was a huge retail store, about 160,000 square feet according to their literature, and featured museum-quality animals in lifelike poses, along with a dizzying array of items for boating, fishing, hunting, camping, hiking and rock climbing. Families went there for a morning or afternoon outing, often eating at the cafeteria and letting their kids loose in their extensive toy section. That Cabela's was the chosen meeting spot was fitting - a larger-than-life store for a larger-than-life dog. Troy had plans to see a football game that day and we were to meet shortly before the game began.

"Can you wait that long?" I asked. Two days can be a long time if one is in a less-than-ideal situation. I worried what other destruction Harley might do in two days.

Troy reassured me that Harley would not be left alone until he turned him back over to me.

After I hung up the phone, I realized that I hadn't mentioned to Troy how sick Olivia was. Adrenaline surged through my body again. Could I manage Harley with Olivia being so sick and needing extra care? Yes, I thought to myself. Perhaps having Harley back would even help Olivia recover.

I called my parents to let them know that Olivia had settled in well, and to share the news about Harley. They were as shocked as I was to hear that the match between Harley and Troy hadn't worked out. We all wondered how this good natured bullmastiff could have done so much damage to Troy's home in such a short time. Both my parents agreed that I had made the right decision to adopt Harley myself. They had grown very attached to him and were looking forward to seeing him again. They offered to take him in whenever I needed to leave the house for work or to take Olivia to the vet.

I then called my brother and told him the news. He reassured me that I would somehow find a way to manage both dogs. We agreed that I could do it, if I just took it one day at a time. After I hung up, I looked over at Olivia. Maybe she could teach Harley the ropes of our schedule. But could I walk both of them together? Clearly Harley needed some leash training. I knew it wouldn't work to leave Harley at home when I took Olivia out. Yet, Harley seemed too excitable to bring along with Olivia for a walk at the same time. I feared that he might bump into her and hurt her unintentionally. These were issues to resolve tomorrow.

Olivia and I prepared to retire for the night. She was clearly exhausted from her full day at the vet's office. Although I was physically tired, my mind was still racing. Harley was coming back! It was hard to believe. Here I'd gone through three days of searching to find Troy, who to all appearances was the perfect match – he had bullmastiff experience, a big house and yard in the country, and a big doggie door - but then after spending $700 for neutering, shots, food, and dog beds, Harley tears up his home, and he wants to return him back to me. I couldn't believe this was happening - this on the very day that Olivia was back at the vet's office with a severe and deteriorating medical condition.

Chapter 14: Saturday November 13th, Learning to Let Go

The next morning I fixed a chicken and rice breakfast for Olivia. This was one of Olivia's favorite treats and I hoped it would entice her to eat. Although she had slept soundly through the night, she still appeared lethargic, unlike her normal self. Disappointingly, she showed no interest in the chicken or even in the venison broth I tried to feed her. I decided to start with the medications instead. First, with a syringe, I squirted medication into her mouth to help coat her stomach. Normally it helps to have a little food in the stomach first, but I had no choice. Then I waited about fifteen minutes. Finally she ate some of the chicken and rice, and I was able to get the rest of the medications successfully into her system by wrapping the pills in chicken.

The phone rang and I quickly rinsed my hands to answer it. Erin from Animal Health Services was checking up on Olivia. I let her know that though Olivia had a rocky start that morning, she had since eaten and taken all her medications. Erin was pleased and we felt hopeful when I hung up.

Suddenly, Olivia rose from her dog bed, hurried outside to a grassy area, and vomited. I watched in horror as she staggered and fell over unconscious. In a panic, I called my father, asking him to rush over to accompany me to the vet. I knew that we only had a short time before Animal Health Services closed at noon. At this point, I didn't care which vet saw her. Looking outside, I saw that Olivia had regained consciousness. She stood up and walked unsteadily back through the open patio door, her tail between her legs. She was clearly weak and seemed more fragile than ever. I helped her over to the dog bed and sat with her, stroking and reassuring her that everything would be alright.

Within minutes, my father arrived and let himself in. I was frantic. I told him I had alerted Animal Health Services and they were waiting for us. I went outside to retrieve a sample of the vomit in case we needed it for testing. To my dismay, I saw that not only had all the medications been regurgitated, but there was blood as well. I quickly gathered up her medications, water and leash. Olivia sat in her dog bed looking up tentatively.

"Olivia, we have to go back to the vet!" I urged.

As I prepared to pick her up, she rose from her bed and walked through the garage to the car. When I opened the door, she hopped in and I joined her in the backseat while my father drove. We stopped by my parent's house to pick up my mother – we all needed to be there if things took a turn for the worse.

We pulled into the Animal Health Services parking lot. Olivia delicately exited the car and walked gingerly to the front door. Although she would have preferred to be at home, she knew we were trying to help her. Once inside, the technician quickly weighed her and guided her to the exam room. She had gained more weight - a sign that she was retaining fluids.

Erin entered the exam room and greeted us, then gave Olivia a sympathetic hug. We were all so grateful to see a familiar face, someone familiar with Olivia's medical history. Unable to contain myself any longer, I burst into tears. I knew Olivia was rapidly losing the battle.

Dr. Wyman entered the exam room and greeted us. Like Dr. DeKing, she was young, perhaps early thirties, medium height, athletic build, with long reddish brown hair. Seeing my tears, she reassured me that she would do everything she could to help Olivia. The examination and blood test revealed that her albumin levels were still low, and that she was very dehydrated. Although Olivia's condition had not improved since yesterday, nor had it substantially declined. Dr. Wyman gave her a shot to help with the vomiting and then telephoned Dr. DeKing for additional counsel. Since the clinic was closing at noon, we were presented with three options. The first was for Olivia to simply return home for rest, but we didn't have a way to provide her with IV fluids. The second was to drive her to the 24-hour emergency clinic, where they could give her IV fluids and keep her stable until Monday. The third was euthanasia. I felt that euthanasia was out of the question, because her condition, though serious, still seemed treatable. Once we could determine what was causing the bleeding, then she could get treatment and she'd be fine. We only needed to keep Olivia stable until Dr. Faver returned on Tuesday.

Feeling uncertain and overwhelmed, I asked to speak with Rob, an experienced practice manager at Animal Health Services. Over the past two years, Rob had been a source of constant emotional support and counsel for Olivia's case. Rob was trained as a veterinarian technician and had a wealth of knowledge from his twenty-plus years of working in the field and at emergency clinics. After reviewing all the options, Rob recommended that we take Olivia to the emergency clinic for fluids, if nothing else. They could get her stabilized until Monday when regular business hours resumed at Animal Health Services. I felt comfortable following his advice. Erin called the clinic so that they would be prepared for us when we arrived.

After riding for what seemed like an eternity, we arrived at the emergency clinic forty minutes away. A technician promptly stepped outside to greet us and help get Olivia safely inside the clinic. Finally, we all gave a big sigh of relief, knowing that this facility was specially equipped to handle severe emergency cases, with the best cutting edge technology and veterinarians skilled in emergency services.

While Olivia was being taken to a back room, I verbally gave the clinic permission to immediately start the IV fluids, and began filling out the paperwork. I showed the technician the medications which had been dispensed to Olivia yesterday, and reminded them that Animal Health Services would be emailing over Olivia's current records from the past two days. Fifteen minutes later, we were taken into an exam room and met with one of the veterinarians assigned to Olivia's case.

The veterinarian reviewed Olivia's case and indicated that because it was very complex, she had to work up a cost estimate for us to review. In summary, we waited over three hours to get a written cost estimate for Olivia's treatment, covering that Saturday afternoon, evening and all of Sunday. The estimate came in at $3,800, not including any surgical procedures. $3,800?!! For what? I also discovered to my horror that during this three hour waiting period, Olivia had just been sitting in a back room of the clinic in a kennel without having been given any IV fluids at all. I was aghast and insisted Olivia be returned to me at once so we could depart the clinic.

The veterinarian returned to the room a few minutes later and offered to cut her estimate by 30 percent. I couldn't believe it. Here she was trying to negotiate money when I had verbally requested and agreed to pay for IV fluids. I called Rob on his cell phone in a panic, letting him know what had happened, and asked if one of the vets from Animal Health Services could come to my house to help Olivia. He agreed, and we quickly loaded Olivia back into the car to head home. At this point, I just wanted her back in a safe and comfortable environment.

Upon returning home, we got Olivia inside and in her dog bed. Over five hours had elapsed and Olivia still had not received any IV fluids. My mother heated some venison broth for her but she still wouldn't eat.

"Rose, Olivia's only chance of recovering from this is to get the next round of medicine in her!" my father said.

My mother and I agreed, but we weren't sure how to do it. Then we remembered that Olivia really liked baby food. Perhaps that would entice her to eat and take her medications. After my father headed out to the store, I saw that Dr. DeKing had left a message. I quickly called her and explained what had happened at the 24-hour emergency clinic. I was still furious at them and distraught over Olivia's condition.

Dr. DeKing and Erin arrived at my house an hour later. They brought IV fluids for Olivia. Even though she was weak, Olivia wagged her tail and greeted them. They took her vital signs and made sure that her lungs were not filling up with fluid. Then they hooked up the IV bag to restore her fluids. We reviewed her medications and the difficulty Olivia was having in taking them. To simplify matters, Dr. DeKing decided to reduce the number of medications, focusing only on the most critical ones to address the bleeding ulcer.

Dr. DeKing understood that we wanted to give Olivia every chance possible to make it. She also understood I was not yet ready to euthanize Olivia. We all agreed to give Olivia a chance to respond to the medication and IV fluids, and then we would recheck her blood on Monday to see how she was responding. The albumin blood results would be the determining factor for whether she should be euthanized. We would do everything we could to stabilize her at home, consistently getting food and medicine in her. I felt better about this decision. We wouldn't euthanize Olivia unless we were 100 percent certain that her condition was declining. There was a glimmer of hope in all of us.

Before she left, Dr. DeKing made it very clear to me to treasure this evening with Olivia, as it might well be her last. Olivia and I were very close and I felt if I lost her I wouldn't know how to go on. She was my rock, my friend and companion. My relationship with her had profoundly affected my life. In my heart, I felt like we were meant to spend many more years together.

After everyone left, I lit some candles, turned on soft music and turned off all the interior lights. This was now going to be a peaceful time for Olivia and me. I lit some dried sage and walked through the house to circulate the scent. Native Americans would use dried sage in various rituals as a means to cleanse a space. Now I used it as a symbol to purify our space after a very stressful day. When Olivia smelled the burning sage- as she had many times before - she let out a soft sigh of relief and tranquility.

That night, I sat outside with Olivia in her dog bed in front of the sliding glass patio door. We inhaled the fragrance of nearby flora and looked up into the desert night sky. This patio and yard had always been our private retreat and safe haven from the world. From the moment we saw this house and yard, I knew that Olivia and I could live here peacefully and harmoniously. It was so unlike our discordant life in Atlanta. I stroked Olivia's fur, grateful for this moment and every moment we had spent together during the last seven years. She had been such a wonderful companion and though her life had been filled with the trauma and stress of being a bait dog, she had never lost her capacity to love. I knew deeply in my heart that I had always done my very best to care for her. We drifted off to sleep in her dog bed, happy to be together in that moment.

Chapter 15: Sunday November 14th, Harley Returns

I woke the next day, filled with confidence and determination. Olivia seemed a little better, a little perkier than the previous night.

"Today's the big day," I thought to myself. "I have to get Olivia up and moving, feed her and get all her medications in her."

This was also the day Harley would return to live with us. I was so excited! I felt certain that if I could get Olivia to take her medications three times today, she would regain enough strength to start her progress toward recovery. And, perhaps even by tomorrow, her albumin levels would start to normalize. Then, once we got the bleeding ulcer repaired, Olivia and I could begin another chapter of our lives with Harley.

Because I wanted to keep an eye on Olivia, I asked my parents if they could meet Troy at Cabela's to pick up Harley later that afternoon. They agreed, and I knew Harley would be glad to see them. They had really bonded in the few days that he was with us.

I waited anxiously with Olivia as the hours passed into early evening. Olivia rested on the sofa while I mused on the unusual circumstances that had intertwined our lives. I was struggling with imagining how our future together would look when the phone rang. It was my mother.

"Well we've got him," my mother exclaimed, "and not only did we get Harley back, we got all his belongings, too!"

My parents picking up Harley at Cabela's

Apparently Troy had packed up everything he had purchased for Harley during the previous week - dog food, containers, a large dog bed, blankets, treats and all of his veterinary records. It was as if an angel had packaged Harley up and sent him back to me with a starter kit!

An hour later, my parents arrived and let themselves in. Harley bounded through the doorway, dragging my father chuckling behind him. Harley hyperventilated with excitement as he caught sight of us, positively elated to be back. After I hugged and kissed him, Harley respectfully approached Olivia who was lying on the sofa and gently touched his nose to hers. He wagged his tail and tenderly sniffed and kissed her with unexpected restraint, perhaps sensing her weakened and fragile state. Olivia responded by sniffing Harley's massive face and wagging her tail with increasing intensity as she happily recognized his scent. After a few minutes of exploring and patrolling around each room of the house, Harley reappeared and settled down on the floor beside the couch, close to Olivia and me, sighing with a deep, sonorous exhalation of utter relief and contentment.

Chapter 16: Monday November 15th, The Decision

After driving my mother home, my father returned and spent Sunday night with Harley in my master bedroom, while I stayed out with Olivia on the sofa. When they woke up, they came out to check on Olivia.

"She was very peaceful and only stirred once during the night." I said. "But she seems a bit lethargic this morning."

Harley softly touched his nose to hers in a good morning sniff to see how she was doing. Olivia wagged her tail weakly, unable to do more, but pleased that Harley was still there.

Today was critical. Later that morning we had an appointment with Dr. DeKing to check Olivia's albumin levels. While I knew that the vet's office would have all the medical resources to help Olivia if she showed improvement, I also feared the worst. The knot in my stomach returned, feeling even tighter than it had on Saturday. I forced myself to concentrate on preparing Olivia's medications and mixing them with chicken and rice baby food. She ate a few spoonfuls and then turned her head, refusing any more.

My mother accompanied me to the vet clinic, while my father stayed behind with Harley. After the preliminaries were dispensed with, Dr. DeKing drew Olivia's blood, taking it to the lab for testing. We waited anxiously in the exam room. I had brought Olivia's bed and blanket to keep her comfortable during the wait. To pass the time and take the edge off our nervousness, my mother and I talked about how Olivia made us smile.

"Remember how when Olivia was younger, she used to love to chase lizards?" my mother reminisced.

Olivia chasing lizards

I remembered. In the backyard, she would catch sight of one and instantly go into alert mode – tail up, eyes transfixed, and body taut in readiness. Then when it moved, she would lunge for it, always missing it by mere inches before it zigzagged away with her in hot pursuit. Invariably the lizard would disappear into a crevice in the backyard wall or into a nearby bush, whereupon Olivia would pace excitedly in front of it, daring the lizard to return. Then she would look at me and lift her paw in full retriever mode, pointing towards the last known location of the lizard, pleading for me to flush it out. As we both laughed at the memory, Olivia looked up at us quizzically.

"Yes, we were talking about you!" I exclaimed.

This seemed to satisfy Olivia and she lay her head down again in her paws.

After an hour, Dr. DeKing returned, a solemn expression on her face.

"Rose, I'm sorry," Dr. DeKing said softly. "The blood work shows Olivia's albumin levels are continuing to drop."

I took a deep breath and wiped tears from my eyes. My mother took my hand in hers consolingly. We glanced at Olivia, unmoving in her dog bed, except for her rib cage rising and falling with each ragged breath. I knew we were losing the battle. Dr. DeKing reviewed our options with us. We could authorize exploratory surgery to attempt to locate and repair the source of the internal bleeding. But, Dr. DeKing warned, given Olivia's age and weakened condition, it would be a slow, painful recovery at best, with a greater likelihood that she simply would not survive the trauma at all. The other option was euthanasia. As painful as it was for me, I chose to have Olivia euthanized right then and there. I knew in my heart that we had to bring an end to her devastating illness and all the complications that had plagued her since she contracted Valley Fever. I did not want her to suffer anymore. I knew the time had come.

In memory of Olivia, November 15, 2010

I held Olivia lovingly in my arms while Dr. DeKing put Olivia to sleep. It happened in seconds, and I felt her warm body gratefully release its last hold on life. I asked Dr. DeKing to save Olivia's ashes for me after her body was cremated.

We drove home in silence, deeply lost in thought, remembering happier times with Olivia. My mother and I were both surprised to feel Olivia's presence still with us in the car on the way home. I kept looking in the back seat to see if somehow we had been mistaken and she had never actually left us. Her presence was so strong in my mind; I felt that even if she wasn't here with us now, her spirit was still alive somewhere, running free and laughing. I smiled as I remembered an earlier time, a defining moment in Olivia's life as a rescue dog.

Mike and I were staying in a cabin in the White Mountain woods in Greer, AZ for a weeklong vacation together. I had Olivia with me – she had been vibrant and healthy at this time – and he had his two labs – Shelby and Samantha, who had helped Olivia work through her fear aggression. Every morning, we would put leashes on the dogs and start the day with a half mile ascent through the forest to the mountain top, occasionally encountering steep passages and challenging terrain – loose rocks and fallen trees blocking our path. Upon reaching the top, a vast clearing greeted us, rewarding our efforts - a picturesque collage of blue sky meeting a green meadow that seemed to extend for miles on end. There, we would unleash the dogs and watch as they ran together as a pack in exhilarating freedom. Their tongues hung from their muzzles as they ran, tails wagging, sometimes catching a scent and trailing it across the field, sometimes just running for the sheer exhilaration of it. As I watched Olivia, I realized then that the abuse and trauma she experienced growing up was gradually becoming a distant memory in her past, being replaced by moments such as these, of the simple consummate joy of being happy, healthy and loved.

When we arrived home, my father and Harley came to greet us. Harley wagged his tail, but seemed surprised that Olivia wasn't with us. He looked at me, tilting his head from side to side inquisitively. He seemed to know that Olivia was gone. My parents patted Harley, gave me a hug, and left, leaving me to sort through the waves of grief and loss that washed over me.

Later that evening, I fixed myself dinner, acutely aware of Olivia's absence in her usual places. We had a routine. In the evenings after dinner, I would sit on one end of the sofa and Olivia would jump on the other, laying her head down in the space between us, often resting it on my lap. Then she would sigh deeply, noisily savoring this sacred moment that was ours, before drifting trustingly off to sleep. Now, as I sat on sofa, I began to cry, feeling the emptiness of loss, feeling alone and betrayed by my unbidden expectations. Suddenly, the sofa shook violently. Harley settled his massive frame awkwardly on the sofa, and gingerly lowered his head onto my leg. Without moving his head, he gazed upwardly into my eyes with a beseechingly sad expression of sympathy. Through tears, I smiled at him and stroked his head as he drooled on my leg. We would get through this together.

Chapter 17: Conclusion of a Miracle

The sequence of events that occurred over the past thirteen days perplexes me even today. From the shock of losing Olivia so suddenly, to the surprise of welcoming Harley back into my home for good, this window in time has been like no other experience I've ever had.

For those of you who wonder how long the bereavement process can take, I have no definitive answer. The time frame differs from person to person, and neither can the process be rushed – each person must fully experience and come to terms with the sorrow of losing his or her beloved companion. When I lost Teela and then Olivia, each time I felt that I could never love another, that no other dog could ever compare. However, I realize now that you can mourn the loss of one dog and still come to love another. I'll admit that if Harley had not come into my life, I may never have understood this. Harley helped me to grieve more and heal faster.

Today Harley and I continue many of the same rituals Olivia and I performed. We have also developed the same closeness. Our daily rhythms are in sync, and the harmony continues to flourish as we live out our daily lives together. We enjoy dog walks almost every day, and we play and relish together the beautiful mysteries life has to offer. Harley and I continue to find serenity in the natural beauty of the high desert. We still visit my parents every day just as Olivia and I did. I still kiss his whiskers and hug him good morning and good night just as I did with Olivia. I miss Teela and Olivia and always will. But in the here and now, in this very special moment in time, Harley and I are together. He is my true friend, companion, and protector.

I am thankful for each day we have together. Remember always that dogs live in the moment of now. They understand that this is all we have. So, even while you plan for the future, enjoy the now while it is here. Please share this true story with any person you know who loves or has ever loved a dog, and know that The Miracle of Harley continues to flourish. There are many other Harley's out there who desperately need homes. Please help these rescue and shelter dogs find their forever homes.

Harley, November 2011

Appendixes

Finding Your Own Harley

When getting a dog, one of the most important factors in establishing a successful pet owner relationship is to make sure that the dog is a good fit with your lifestyle and living situation. Consider whether you want a purebred or a mixed breed dog. Different breeds have different traits that strongly influence their behavior and needs, on such aspects as the amount of exercise, obedience training, and grooming needed. Consider what type of characteristics you are looking for in a dog – activity level, temperament, size, coat. Consider whether you want a puppy or an adult dog. Puppies offer the advantage of being trainable from a young age, and allow you to foster behaviors that will be suitable for your family and lifestyle. But this training can be very labor intensive. Older dogs often come with some foundation of obedience training, and may have an easier time adjusting to your household rules. Depending upon what type of dog you are planning to take in, you'll be faced with different issues and challenges. Educate yourself. Read books, research websites, attend dog shows, visit local shelters, talk to breeders, and most of all, try to anticipate the issues that may arise. Below are some general questions to help you think about issues involved in bringing a dog into your home.

1. How much space do you have for the dog? How large is your house? How large is your yard? If you do not have a yard, how will you provide the dog the necessary walks for exercise and for elimination? What determines the amount of exercise needed is not necessarily the dog's size, but rather their activity level. For example, some small dogs, such as the Jack Russell terrier, tend to be extremely active dogs that need a lot of exercise and room to run around. Some larger dogs, such as greyhounds, are less active and need only brief amounts of exercise. Dogs that have inadequate space to exercise may respond with destructive behavior. Dogs that have lots of space, and/or are given lots of exercise tend to be better balanced.

2. If you are considering getting a puppy, what type of knowledge and experience have you had with puppies? Puppies often require very specialized care during their

early months, in terms of potty training, obedience training, and redirecting puppy and/or breed-specific behaviors such as chewing or digging.

3. How will the dog be received by the other members of your family? If you have children, especially small children, how compatible will this breed's temperament be towards them? For example, Golden and Labrador Retrievers are well-known for their gentle dispositions.

4. What is your financial situation and will you be able to afford it? Owning a dog can cost from $700-$3000 per year, or an average of $90-$200 per month, depending on several key factors: the dog's size, health, grooming needs, and possible pet-sitting/boarding needs.

   The size of the dog will affect the food and veterinary costs. A small dog weighing up to ten pounds will probably eat approximately ¼ to ¾ of dry dog food per day. A larger dog weighing 75 pounds or more will eat 2-4 cups per day, approximately five to eight times more food than a smaller dog. Dogs with allergies may need to eat more specialized dog food, adding to the expense.

   The cost of some common preventative medicines may also vary according to the size of your dog. For example, the dosage for heartworm medication is determined by how much the dog weighs, and can be as much as 50% more expensive for a large 100 pound dog than for a small 20 pound dog ($60/year supply vs. $90/year supply)

   Grooming is another factor. Dog's nails need to be trimmed about every three to four weeks, something you can do yourself, or have done as a service. Some dogs, such as poodles and shih-tzus, need to be brought to a groomer to have their fur trimmed every five to eight weeks.

   Boarding and pet sitting are other possible expenses, depending upon your work schedule. For example, you might need to hire a pet sitter to walk or feed your dog if you are away from for an extended period of time. If you travel out of town, you will need to make arrangements for your dog to be cared for in your absence.

Veterinary care and licensing are other regular expenses. Most vets recommend your dog receive yearly medical check-ups and vaccinations as needed. Most cities or counties require that the dog's rabies vaccination be regularly updated and registered with the district or municipality. When you first get your dog, you may incur additional expenses cover the cost of vaccinations, spaying or neutering, heart worm tests and medication, and addressing other possible medical conditions.

5. What types of obedience training are available in your community? Many national stores such as Petco and PetSmart offer reliable, quality obedience training. Other local obedience training may be available in your community. Ask your vet for a recommendation.

Where to find your dog

Once you have decided that you want to get a dog, you have several options for where to get one. For purebred dogs, research breed clubs to find a reputable breeder who is willing to talk to you about the breed you are considering. Breed rescue is often a good source for finding an adult dog. Many breed rescues use foster homes, so they know a lot about the dogs they are re-homing. If you prefer a mixed breed dog, contact local rescue agencies and shelters. If you are not sure what kind of dog you would like, or want to test the waters before actually getting a dog, consider fostering. Fostering can be a great way to help dogs and to discover what kind of dog suits you. You get a chance to re-home needy dogs or to find one that is a great match for you. Avoid pet stores, and backyard breeders. Be wary of ads offering to bring a puppy to you - these are often puppy mill puppies.

How to select your dog

In selecting your dog, keep in mind the traits you are looking for. If a dog doesn't seem quite right, don't get it. Know your limitations in terms of finances, time, and energy. Don't let looks sway you. A dog should appeal to you, but looks aren't everything.

Ideally you want to get a well-socialized dog, one that seems to take things in stride and doesn't over-react to things in its environment. Spend time with the dog or puppy you have initially selected and observe its temperament and how it responds to you. Is it curious or shy? Dogs that are curious and interact with you may be better socialized, and may get along better with other people and other dogs. Always take into consideration the dog's breed traits. Bassett hounds, for example, tend to hold back more and take everything in before reacting, and may come across as shy, when in fact they are not.

Whether you are at an animal shelter, or a rescue organization, most of these staff members conduct an assessment to find out if the dog is compatible with small children or cats. So, be sure to ask the staff about compatibility, and request any other information that they may have about the dog you are interested in adopting.

A purebred dog

If you are thinking of purchasing a purebred dog or purebred puppy, ask yourself and your family the questions below. If you are still not sure about the pros and cons of getting a purebred dog, discuss the options with your vet or a breeder you are considering. Breeders are usually very willing to meet with prospective owners to help inform them about the breed. Being able to meet the dogs "parents" is extremely beneficial because you will get to see their disposition, and the disposition that your dog is likely to inherit. When you purchase from an out-of-state breeder, you may be inadvertently purchasing from a puppy mill.

1. What do you know about the breed you are considering? What are the specific breed behaviors that might make this dog a challenge for you to take care of, or may impact the suitability of bringing the dog into your home? How realistic are your expectations of this breed? Some examples of characteristics to look for are digging, herding, strong propensity for barking or howling, scent tracking, strong protective instincts, high level needs for companionship, etc.

2. What is the energy level of this breed, and will you be able to provide the necessary amount of exercise? For example, Australian shepherds are high-energy dogs that are bred for herding sheep, and require a lot of exercise and mental stimulation. So if you select a high-energy, high-activity level dog, make sure that your own energy level and lifestyle are a suitable match.

3. What climate is most suitable for the breed you are considering? For example, if you live in a hot climate, a dog with thick, heavy fur such as a husky or a Saint Bernard might have difficulty tolerating hot weather.

A rescue dog

Dogs that are being cared for or fostered by a rescue group are dogs whose previous owners can no longer care for them. Rescue groups are usually breed-specific, taking in dogs of only one particular breed. These breed-specific rescue groups are familiar with the history, the characteristics, traits, and special needs of the breed. These groups are also familiar with some of the genetic faults and medical problems that are common to the breed. In most cases, these rescue groups have an entire support system of individuals who can temporarily take care of the dogs or puppies until a proper home is found. Rescue groups are staffed by volunteers who understand the types of situations rescue dogs can emerge from, such as a Great Dane puppy who grew into a really big dog and the owners decided the dog was too large for them to keep in their one bedroom apartment. These volunteers can help ensure a good match and a good fit between you and your new dog.

A shelter dog

Shelter dogs are often brought in by animal control, or by people in the community who have found stray or unwanted dogs. Some shelters are no-kill shelters; others keep dogs for only a limited amount of time, after which these animals are euthanized. Shelters are also staffed by volunteers who have extensive experience in not only assessing the temperament of the dog, but also the needs of the potential owner, so that the best match can be made. They can help direct you to the dog whose needs and temperament will be best suited to your home and lifestyle. When looking for a dog in a shelter, here are some questions to keep in mind.

- How is the dog's temperament? Does he seem relaxed and friendly, or shy and anxious? The degree of shyness may be an indication of how well socialized the dog is. Keep in mind that a dog that seems shy or anxious may be simply responding to the stressful kennel environment. Once away from this environment and in your home, the dog may exhibit much more relaxed and socialized behaviors.

- What information do you have about the dog's history? Find out as much as you can from either the rescue or shelter group.

- What special needs might the dog have? Consider things such as exercise, obedience training, and any special medical conditions.

- If you have other pets at home, how will the dog be received, and how will the dog react to these other pets? Rescue and shelter groups should be able to tell you if the dog will be suitable for a household with other dogs or cats.

- If you have children, how will the dog behave towards them?

Before Bringing Your Dog Home

Before bringing your dog home, think about special items that he or she will need. Make sure that your home is safe for your dog, and plan for how you want him or her to behave in your home.

1. Purchase dog items such as a bed, toys, a crate and leash. Make sure that the crate is the right size for your dog. Your local store should be able to assist you with this based on the breed, height, weight, and age.

2. Dog proof your home. Be sure that food items and harmful items, such as household chemicals, are not accessible.

3. Think about boundaries in your home. For example, if you will allow your dog on furniture, make sure you have washable coverings. If your dog is not to be allowed upstairs, get a baby gate to block access to the upper floor.

4. Find out about your community. Does your dog need to have a license? What are the leash laws? Are there any dog parks? Where are the local veterinary clinics?

Bringing Your Dog Home

When you first bring your dog home, keep the environment calm. Don't invite everyone over to meet your new friend yet. Give the dog some time to acclimate to its new home.

1. Establish routines right away. Keep a consistent schedule for meals and regular walks. You may need to walk your dog more frequently the first few days while he gets adjusted to his new environment.

2. Initially, you may want to limit the dog's access to all areas of your home, because this will help with housebreaking.

3. Establish limits, and adopt behaviors that show your dog that you are the leader. For example, teach your dog to wait for you to go through the door first. Have the dog sit or wait before you feed her.

4. Enroll your dog in an obedience class. These classes are a great way to help establish a bond with your dog. Dog agility classes are a great way to build a bond with shy dogs, and helps build their confidence.

5. Be aware that there is usually a "honeymoon" period with a new dog. Your dog may seem perfect at first, but as she becomes more secure in her new home, she may begin to show more of her true personality. Establishing routines and limits and enrolling in an obedience class should help prevent any serious issues.

What to Do if You Find a Lost Dog

If you come across a dog that seems to be lost, you can play an instrumental role in helping to reunite the dog with its owner.

1. First, check the dog to see if she has a collar or identity tags. If you are lucky, these tags will have the owner's contact information so that you can contact them immediately. See if the dog has any other form of identification such as a municipal dog license number, or a rabies tag. If yes, you can contact the association where she is registered to find the owner's contact information.

2. If the owner's information is not available, check to see if the dog is wounded or appears to be in physical distress. If so, and if you feel comfortable doing so, bring it immediately to the nearest vet.

3. If the dog is not wounded or distressed, bring him into a safe place in your home or yard and give him some water. Be sure the dog is out of extreme weather conditions such as excessive heat or extreme cold.

4. Call the local police or sheriff to see if anyone has reported a lost dog.

5. The dog may have a microchip containing information about the dog's owner. If you feel comfortable with the dog, take him to a vet clinic or 24 hour emergency clinic and have him scanned for a microchip. If the dog has a microchip, the vet clinic will help contact the owner.

6. If the dog has no identity tags, the dog may live locally in the area, having escaped from its house or yard. In order to help find this owner, photograph the dog, and create a flyer with the dog's photo, a brief description, and where he was found. Print and post these flyers on mailboxes or street posts near where you found the missing pet. See the http://www.bestfriends.org for a sample flyer.

7. Contact a local vet, and have them disseminate the information about the lost dog to local rescue groups.

8. Email, text, tweet, post on Facebook, and call as many people, friends and neighbors as possible.

9. If you cannot care for the dog, call and make arrangements with a local rescue group or animal shelter.

Fostering a Rescue Dog

The need for fostering rescue dogs is enormous. When a rescue dog is brought into a foster home, it increases their chances for adoption by approximately thirty percent. The foster dog home environment typically offers the rescue dog a chance to rehabilitate from its past trauma, medical neglect, and emotional abandonment. If you feel you and your family may be candidates for this type of commitment, please contact rescue groups in your area. They will provide you with the necessary training and orientation. This experience can change your life.

Glossary of Terms

Albumin levels Albumin is protein created in the liver. Abnormally low ranges are seen with diseased livers and gastrointestinal diseases. The only time albumin is increased is when the animal is dehydrated. Albumin helps keep the liquid part (plasma) of the blood from migrating out of the blood vessels and into the surrounding tissues, which would cause edema and other problems. Side note: Olivia was losing albumin because of the bleeding in her stomach. This caused albumin to be pulled into her digestive system and eliminated through her feces.

Animal rescue Operations or efforts made by a person or group to save an animal's life.

Animal shelters Organizations that provide a temporary safe place of refuge for the animal. Food, water and shelter are provided. If animals are not adopted, they may be euthanized. Some shelters, called no-kill shelters, are committed to finding a home for the animal, ensuring that none of the animals are euthanized. Animal shelters often take in animals that are confiscated from animal hoarders. Animal hoarders have a condition recognized by the medical profession as a psychiatric disease that is closely related to obsessive compulsive disorder where the person compulsively collects animals as their pets, often beyond their means, putting the animals' health and well-being at risk.

Backyard breeders Individuals or groups of people who breed dogs, usually purebred dogs, as a for-profit business, where profit takes priority over the animal's well-being. These breeders often put ads in newspapers, sell animals over the internet and even sell to pet stores. These animals are often inbred, have shorter lifespans and are stricken with many breed-specific illnesses.

Bait dog A dog that is used to test another dog's fighting instinct. The bait dog is usually mauled or killed in the process.

Baiting or dog baiting The act of setting game dogs against a chained or confined animal for sport. The dogs bite to subdue the opposing animal by incapacitating or killing it. Baiting is a blood sport used for entertainment and gambling, and is illegal in most countries, including the United States.

Breed specific dogs These dogs are purebred dogs such as Golden Retrievers, Poodles, etc.

Conscious proprioception A condition of not knowing where the feet are, a common problem associated with older dogs that have arthritis of the spine causing swelling and irritation of their spinal cord. Though not painful, dogs often have limited ability to control their legs on slick flooring surfaces. If they have solid footing or some form of traction on the floor, they usually can function adequately. This condition may be eased but not eliminated by prescribed anti-inflammatory medication.

Dog crate A completely enclosed cage-like structure made of sturdy wire with a closeable gate to allow entry and exit. Ideally the crate should be large enough for the dog to turn around comfortably.

Dog pound An older, more outdated term, more commonly referred to now as an animal shelter. See *animal shelter*.

Euthanasia A medical procedure performed by a veterinarian to terminate the life of an animal painlessly.

Forever home A term used by animal rescue workers, shelter workers and foster dog parents to describe a safe, happy, and loving permanent environment for rescued dogs to live out their lives.

Fighting dogs Dogs that are trained to fight other dogs as part of a gambling, spectator sport.

Foster dogs Dogs that are temporarily cared for by a foster parent - someone who agrees to help rehabilitate the dog emotionally and/or physically so that the dog may be successfully adopted.

Homeless dogs Any dog that does not have a permanent home.

Humane societies Organizations devoted to promoting humane ideals, especially in regards to the treatment of animals.

Laryngeal paralysis A condition that affects the larynx, where the muscles that control the larynx suffer from paralysis, impairing the dog's ability to breathe, making the dog very anxious. The more difficult the breathing, the more anxious the dog becomes, leading to more rapid breathing and more distress. A respiratory crisis from the partial obstruction can emerge, creating an emergency and even death. The condition is usually gradual, and symptoms include excess panting, exercise intolerance, loud breathing signs, and gasping for breath. Dogs most susceptible to this condition are older large-breed dogs, most commonly Labrador Retrievers.

Owner surrender When an owner legally relinquishes ownership of the dog by turning it over to a rescue group. The rescue group will most likely have the owner sign a surrender form that gives the rescue group ownership of the dog.

Pack leader A term popularized by Cesar Milan, the host of the television show "The Dog Whisperer," representing someone who sets rules, boundaries, and limitations for the pack, and in so doing, nurtures the dog's healthy state of mind.

Puppy mills and factory farms A puppy mill is a breeding facility with the sole purpose of breeding the maximum number of dogs for the lowest expense possible to make the most profit. Puppy mills and factory farms often use substandard breeding conditions and inbreeding, which can lead to genetic health problems. These dogs often suffer from behavioral issues as well, as a result of being taken from their mothers too soon, resulting in development and socialization difficulties and serious behavioral problems later in life.

Rescue dogs Dogs that have been placed in a new home after being abused, neglected, or abandoned by its previous owner.

Dogs adopted from rescue organizations are often referred to as rescue dogs. Some rescue dogs never go to shelters.

Separation anxiety A condition where the dog experiences extreme anxiety when left alone. This anxiety may manifest itself through continual howling, barking or crying, or through varying degrees of destruction to the home, crate, yard or environment in which they are left.

Shelters An establishment, especially one supported by charitable contributions, that provides a temporary home for dogs, cats, and other animals that are offered for adoption.

Shelter dogs Dogs adopted from shelters are often referred to as shelter dogs.

Titer A titer is a blood test which uses a serial dilution technique to measure the level of antibodies that the body has produced. These antibodies are the body's response to the disease or antigens (protein from the actual disease organism virus, fungal, etc.) and are used to evaluate the severity of disease. In the case of Valley Fever, the titer measures the antibodies produced by the body in response to the fungus.

Valley Fever (Coccidiodomycosis) This is a fungal infection, caused by the Coccidioides immitis fungus spores. This condition is common in the Southwest desert regions of the United States. The spores reside in the soil, and when soil is disturbed, the spores become airborne. The spores can live for a long time in harsh environmental conditions such as heat, cold and drought. People and animals with weakened immune systems are often more susceptible to the disease. The fungus can cause skin ulcers, abscesses, bone lesions, severe joint pain, heart inflammation, urinary track problems, meningitis, secondary infections and often death. According to The University of Arizona Valley Fever Center for Excellence, dogs in Arizona have a 28 percent chance of contracting Valley Fever by the age of two. Of these dogs, 6 percent will show signs of clinical illness within two years. The Veterinary Specialty Center of Tucson offers clinical Valley Fever research in companion animals. For more information, go to their website at: http://www.vfce.arizona.edu/Default.aspx.

General Resources

American Animal Health Association (AAHA)
http://www.aaha.net.org

> AAHA is an organization that has developed a set of accreditation standards that are widely used as benchmarks for measuring excellence in veterinary care, allowing animal hospitals to demonstrate the quality of their care to the communities and clients they serve. Currently, more than 3,200 veterinary clinics are certified with the "AAHA-accredited" designation.

American Bullmastiff Association Rescue Service (ABARS) http://bullmastiff.us/rescue

> This organization's mission is to find forever homes for unwanted bullmastiffs that come from shelters, or who are owner-surrendered from people who, for whatever **reason**, are no longer able to keep the dog, even if the dog was purchased from a pet shop or a backyard breeder. Surrendered bullmastiffs are neutered or spayed before they are adopted. They receive thorough veterinary care before any adoptions take place. Adoption forms and owner-surrender forms are available on the website. The "Available Rescue Dogs" link shows the bullmastiffs needing forever homes. Keep in mind the unique challenges of owning and caring for this breed, as is indicated in the "about bullmastiffs" section.

The American Society for the Prevention of Cruelty to Animals (ASPCA) http://www.aspca.org

> The ASPCA was the first humane society to be established in North America, founded in 1866. Their headquarters is located in New York City. Their website has lists and guidelines of how to recognize and report animal cruelty to local officials in your area. Complaints about animal cruelty and fighting can be reported to the ASPCA Humane Law Enforcement at (212) 867-7700,

extension 4450, or email *humane1@aspca.org*, or report the incidence to your local police. On-site training for law enforcement training and questions may be emailed to lobby@aspca.org. The ASPCA also has an Animal Poison Control Center 24-hour hotline at **(888)** 426-4435, and monitors pet food recalls, market withdrawals and safety alerts for animals. Mobile phone apps and email alerts are available at http://www.fda.gov/Safety/Recalls

Animal Health Services Surgical and Diagnostic Center
http://www.ahsvet.com

This veterinary clinic is AAHA-accredited, and is currently a 24 hour, urgent and critical care center located in Cave Creek, Arizona (480 488-6181).

Best Friends Animal Society http://www.bestfriends.org

Best Friends operates the nation's largest sanctuary for homeless animals and provides a variety of services: adoption, spaying and neutering, and educational programs. Best Friends operates an interactive online global community, the "Best Friends Network" (http://network.bestfriends.org). They also publish the nation's largest general-interest animal magazine. Their website provides an excellent downloadable guide *"Best Friends' ABCs of Dog Life,"* containing invaluable information for anyone who decides to get a dog.

Care Credit (http://www.carecredit.com/vetmed/)

This organization, part of GE Capital, offers healthcare financing for pets, and has a network of over 150,000 providers. Some of these providers practice veterinary medicine. Care Credit allows consumers to apply for credit with many different payment options.

The Humane Society of the United States
http://www.hsus.org

HSUS, located in Washington DC, was established in 1954 and is presently the nation's largest and oldest animal protection organization, advocating for local humane societies across the country. The HSUS has over 11 million American members. They provide standards to help monitor the quality of care provided by shelters, evaluations, training programs, and national advertising campaigns to promote pet adoption, direct support, and national conferences. Their magazine, available at http://www.animalsheltering.org/magazine, contains stories about the work that they do.

The American Kennel Club http://www.akc.org

The AKC offers information on dog breeds, competition events, club search for training and services, dog ownership and registration to help you discover more about the joys of having a dog.

The National Council On Pet Overpopulation Study And Policy (NCPPSP) http://www.petpopulation.org

This organization's mission is to gather and analyze reliable data on the number, origin, and disposition of pets in the United States, to promote responsible stewardship of companion animals, and to recommend programs to reduce the number of homeless pets in the United States.

People for the Ethical Treatment Of Animals (PETA)
http://peta.org

Located in Norfolk, Virginia, it was founded in 1980 as a non-profit organization. With over two million members and supporters, it is reputed to be the largest animal rights organization in the world.

Petfinder Foundation http://www.petfinderfoundation.com

This foundation provides support to shelters, rescue organizations and animal welfare organizations across the United States in the form of funding, training, and education. Their mission is to help ensure that no adoptable pet is euthanized for lack of a good home. As part of this mission, they maintain an extensive database of homeless pets linked to more than 13,500 animal welfare organizations nationwide. Their database, at http://www.petfinder.com, allows people to search online for available dogs.

The University of Arizona Valley Fever Center For Excellence http://www.vfce.arizona.edu

Their website contains a link for "Valley Fever in Dogs." The Veterinary Specialty Center of Tucson is the hub for their Valley Fever research studies, providing current research findings as well as access to support groups.

Pet Loss and Pet Loss Support Groups

Association for Pet Loss and Bereavement (APLB)
http://www.aplb.org

> The ASPCA has grief counseling for people grieving the loss of a companion animal. They also offer assistance in deciding whether to euthanize or not. The ASPCA Pet Loss Hotline is (877)-GRIEF-10.

American Society for Prevention of Cruelty to Animals (ASPCA) http://www.aspca.org

> The ASPCA has grief counseling for people grieving the loss of a companion animal. They also offer assistance with the decision to euthanize. The ASPCA Pet Loss Hotline is (877)-GRIEF-10.

Local vets

> Grief counseling is often available from local vets on a request basis.

Recommended Reading

Becker, Marty Dr., with Morton, Danelle, The Healing Power of Pets: Harnessing the Amazing Ability of Pets to Make and Keep People Happy and Healthy. New York, NY: Hyperion, 2002.

Glen, Samantha, and Mary Tyler Moore. Best Friends: The True Story of the World's Most Beloved Animal Sanctuary. New York, NY: Kensington, 2001.

Gorant, Jim, The Lost Dogs: Michael Vick's Dogs and Their Tale of Redemption. New York, NY: Gotham Books, 2010.

Knapp, Caroline. Pack of Two: The Intricate Bond between People and Dogs. New York, NY: Dial, 1998.

Levin, Larry. Oogy: The Dog Only a Family Could Love. New York: Grand Central Pub., 2010.

Millan, Cesar, and Melissa Jo. Peltier. Cesar's Way: The Natural, Everyday Guide to Understanding and Correcting Common Dog Problems. New York: Harmony, 2006.

Sheldrake, Rupert. Dogs That Know When Their Owners Are Coming Home: and Other Unexplained Powers of Animals. New York: Crown, 1999.

Sife, Wallace. The Loss of a Pet. New York: Howell Book House, 1993.

Thomas, Elizabeth Marshall. The Hidden Life of Dogs. Boston: Houghton Mifflin, 1993.

Thomas, Elizabeth Marshall. The Social Lives of Dogs: The Grace of Canine Company. New York: Simon & Schuster, 2000.

Acknowledgements

My deep gratitude and appreciation to the following people and associations for helping me to care for Olivia and to share this story of the Miracle of Harley. These acknowledgements are in no particular order.

To Animal Health Services, including all veterinarians, veterinarian assistants and staff for their passionate commitment to all the animals they treat in their practice, and especially for their special love and care for Olivia during her devastating illnesses.

To all rescue workers and rescue groups who spend their time, energy and financial resources rescuing animals.

To Elizabeth, for her invaluable insight as editor, and in helping me to articulate the story that I was compelled to write.

To Yon, for his invaluable insight as editor and relentless dedication to perfecting this story of The Miracle of Harley.

To Sarah Whiting, for her contributing idea of adding the *Finding Your Own Harley* section to this book.

To Dawn and Virginia for their commitments to American Bullmastiff Association Rescue Service.

To Dr. DeKing, for her compassionate care, commitment, and wise veterinary counsel in treating Olivia during her final days.

To Dr. Faver for his unending care and medical supervision of Olivia's complex case history, and to the integrity he contributes to his profession.

To Dr. Wyman, for her compassionate ability to help Olivia when she was in a severe medical crisis.

To Dr. Lannen, for her ability to recognize all of Olivia's debilitating medical signs of Valley Fever.

To Erin, for her outstanding ability in treating Olivia during her most difficult time.

To Bobby, for her kindness and care of Olivia throughout the course of her various treatments.

To Rob, for his kind words and assistance when there was no one else to turn to.

To Mom and Dad, for their unyielding love and commitment in all that I have pursued in my life; especially dog love.

To my brother Dan, for his wise counsel and helping me see that Harley and I were meant to live together.

To my sister-in-law, Ellen, for her infinite patience in accepting oversized dogs who drool into her life.

To my nephews, Warren and Wallace, for their love of the mastiff and bullmastiff breed.

To Georgia (Ann), for finding Olivia.

To Bill, for allowing me to lead the efforts to find Harley a new home.

To Melissa, for creating the photographic essence of what a miracle can look like.

To Sue, for encouraging me to continue writing even when I felt I couldn't complete the story.

To Rhonda, for connecting me to Bill and Harley.

To Jeserae (Sarah), for photographing and text messaging when we were trying to find Harley a home.

To Amy, for encouraging me to write about Olivia's bait dog history.

To Bruce L., for inspiring me to write about dogs twenty-five years ago, even before I recognized that I could.

To Shelby, Samantha, and Mike for helping to rehabilitate Olivia.

To all the people and rescue groups who called, emailed, and texted about Harley.

To Mark, for helping to educate me on the large mastiff breed.

To Ikon, for teaching me that there are dogs bigger than Harley.

To Teela, for spending sixteen wonderful years with me.

To Coco, for helping me fall in love with the mastiff breed.

To Olivia, for teaching me that I could love another dog who needed a home.

To Harley, for reminding all of us that miracles are possible, and that countless rescue and shelter dogs need forever homes.

To God, and all higher powers, from which countless miracles evolve.

About the Author

Rose M. Murphy is a nationally certified commercial interior designer and author. She received a Bachelor of Fine Arts in Interior Design, College of Visual and Performing Arts, from Syracuse University. She has thirty years professional experience working in residential and commercial sectors as a design consultant, critic and coach. She is a published author in her design profession. Personally, she actively contributes as a rescue dog worker, and as an advocate for helpless, homeless, and abused dogs.

If you would like to share the story about your rescue dog with other readers, please send it to the attention of Harley at zdogzpublishingllc@gmail.com or mail it to zDogz Publishing, LLC, 39506 North Daisy Mountain Drive, Suite 122- No. 261, Anthem, Arizona 85086. Selected stories will be posted onto the Miracle of Harley's website at http://www.miracleofharley.com.

www.ingramcontent.com/pod-product-compliance
Lightning Source LLC
Chambersburg PA
CBHW071006040426
42443CB00007B/685